AN AGE OF EMPIRES, 1200–1750

BONNIE G. SMITH

GENERAL EDITOR

AN AGE OF EMPIRES, 1200–1750

Marjorie Wall Bingham

To Thomas Egan, my husband and colleague

OXFORD
UNIVERSITY PRESS

Oxford University Press, Inc., publishes works that further
Oxford University's objective of excellence
in research, scholarship, and education.

Oxford New York
Auckland Cape Town Dar es Salaam Hong Kong Karachi
Kuala Lumpur Madrid Melbourne Mexico City Nairobi
New Delhi Shanghai Taipei Toronto

With offices in
Argentina Austria Brazil Chile Czech Republic France Greece
Guatemala Hungary Italy Japan Poland Portugal Singapore
South Korea Switzerland Thailand Turkey Ukraine Vietnam

Published by Oxford University Press, Inc.
198 Madison Avenue, New York, New York 10016
www.oup.com

Design: Stephanie Blumenthal and Alexis Siroc
Cover design and logo: Nora Wertz

Library of Congress Cataloging-in-Publication Data

Bingham, Marjorie Wall.
An age of empires, 1200–1750 / Marjorie Wall Bingham.
p. cm. — (Medieval & early modern world)
ISBN-13: 978-0-19-517839-5 — 978-0-19-522268-5 (Calif. ed.) — 978-0-19-522157-2 (set)
ISBN-10: 0-19-517839-4 — 0-19-522268-7 (Calif. ed.) — 0-19-522157-5 (set)
1. Middle Ages—History--Juvenile literature. 2. History, Modern—16th century—Juvenile literature.
3. History, Modern—17th century—Juvenile literature. 4. History, Modern—18th century—Juvenile literature.
5. Imperialism—History—Juvenile literature. 6. Militarism—History—Juvenile literature.
I. Title. II. Medieval and early modern world.
D202.B46 2005
909.07--dc22
2004030009

9 8 7 6 5 4 3 2 1

Printed in the United States of America on acid-free paper

On the cover: A bronze water vessel from Saxony, a region in Germany, takes the shape of an armored knight atop his horse.
Frontispiece: The Turkish army of sultan Mehmet II lays siege to the Greek island of Rhodes in the 15th century.

BONNIE G. SMITH
GENERAL EDITOR

DIANE L. BROOKS, Ed. D.
EDUCATION CONSULTANT

The European World, 400–1450
Barbara A. Hanawalt

The African and Middle Eastern World, 600–1500
Randall L. Pouwels

The Asian World, 600–1500
Roger V. Des Forges and John S. Major

An Age of Empires, 1200–1750
Marjorie Wall Bingham

An Age of Voyages, 1350–1600
Merry E. Wiesner-Hanks

An Age of Science and Revolutions, 1600–1800
Toby E. Huff

The Medieval and Early Modern World: Primary Sources & Reference Volume
Donald R. Kelley and Bonnie G. Smith

CONTENTS

A [“] marks a primary source—a piece of writing that speaks to us from the past.

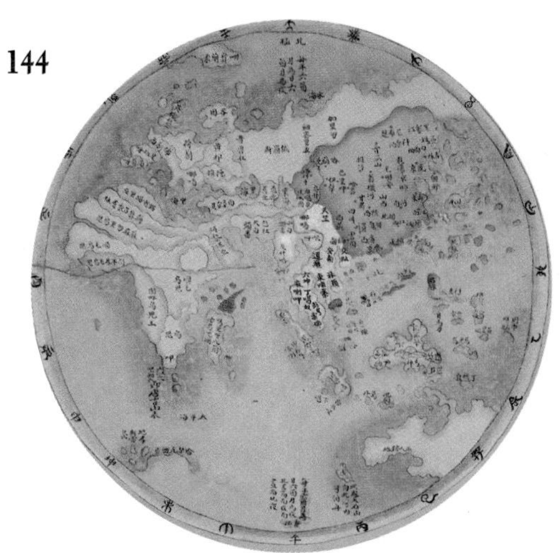

CAST OF CHARACTERS

Ahmet III (ah-MEHT), 1673–1736 • Ottoman sultan of Tulip Era

Akbar (AHK-bahr), ruled 1556–1605 • Mughal emperor at height of empire

Alexis 1629–1676 • Russian tsar who began Westernization

Aurangzeb (oh-rahng-ZEHB), 1618–1707 • Last of major Mughal rulers

Babur (BAH-bur), 1483–1530 • Founder of Mughal Empire

Balboa (bal-BOH-uh), **Vasco de** (VAS-ko deh), 1475–1519 • Spaniard who led first European expedition to western Pacific Ocean

Batu (bah-TOO), ?–1255 • Mongol leader of Golden Horde that controlled Russia

Beyazit (bay-AH-zeet), **the Thunderbolt,** 1360–1403 • Sultan who established Ottoman foothold in Europe

Camoes (cah-MOYSH), **Luis de** (loo-EES deh), 1515–80 • Author of *The Luciads*, epic of Portuguese exploration

Cervantes (sehr-VAHN-tess), **Miguel de** (mee-GEHL deh) 1547–1616 • Spanish author of *Don Quixote*

Charles V, ruled 1519–56 • German emperor and (as Charles I) king of Spain

Columbus, Christopher, 1451–1506 • Italian explorer, leader of first-known Europeans to reach Americas since Vikings

Copernicus (kuh-PER-nih-kuhs), **Nicolaus,** 1473–1543 • Polish astronomer who advanced understanding of the solar system

Cortés (kor-TEHZ), **Hernán** (ehr-NAHN), 1485–1547 • Spanish explorer, conqueror of Mexica (Aztec) Empire

da Gama (duh GAH-mah), **Vasco** (VAS-ko), 1469–1524 • Portuguese captain who reached India by sailing around Africa

Dias (DEE-ush), **Bartolomeu** (bahr-TAHL-AH-mew), 1450?–1500 • Portuguese captain who rounded southern tip of Africa

Eugene of Savoy, 1663–1736 • Habsburg general who led army against Ottomans

Ferdinand of Aragon, 1452–1516 • Joint ruler of Spain with Isabella

Genghis Khan (Temujin) (GENG-guhs KAHN), 1167–1227 • Mongol conqueror of largest land empire ever

Henry the Navigator, 1394–1460 • Portuguese prince who supported navigation and trade

Isabella of Castile, 1451–1504 • Joint ruler of Spain with Ferdinand

Ivan the Terrible, 1530–84 • Tsar of Russia who defeated Tartars and extended Russia into Siberia

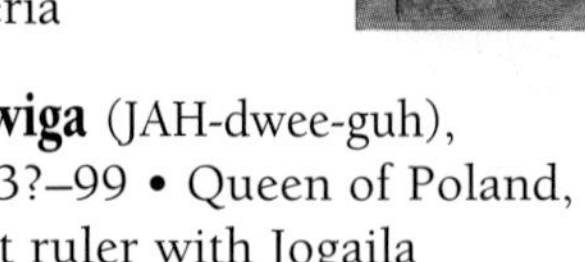

Jadwiga (JAH-dwee-guh), 1373?–99 • Queen of Poland, joint ruler with Jogaila

Jogaila (JOH-gai-luh), 1351–1434 • King of Poland and Lithuania, ruled with Jadwiga

Kangxi (kahng-shee), 1661–1722 • Qing emperor of China

Kepler, Johannes, 1571–1630 • Habsburg astronomer, discovered elliptical planetary movements

Khubilai Khan (KOO-buh-lie KAHN), 1215–94 • Mongol ruler of China in Yuan dynasty

Magellan (muh-JEHL-an), **Ferdinando,** 1480?–1521 • Portuguese captain who led first expedition to circumnavigate the globe though he was killed part of the way through

Maria Theresa, 1717–80 • Habsburg ruler who began reforming the military and tax and education systems

Mehmet (meh-MEHT) **II the Conqueror,** 1432–81 • Ottoman sultan who conquered Constantinople

Moctezuma II (MOKE-teh-zoo-mah), 1467–1520 • Mexica (Aztec) emperor

Nur Jahan (NOOR juh-HAHN), 1577–1645 • Wife of Mughal leader Jahangir, who ruled in his name

Peter the Great, 1672–1725 • Tsar of Russia who founded St. Petersburg

Philip II, 1527–98 • King of Spain, sent the Armada to attack England

Pizarro (puh-ZAHR-oh), **Francisco** (frahn-SIS-ko), 1478?–1541 • Spanish conqueror of Inca Empire

Polo, Marco 1253?–1324 • Venetian merchant who traveled to China during Khubilai Khan's era

Qianlong (chyen-loong), 1736–96 • Qing emperor of China

Selim (seh-LEEM) **the Grim,** ruled 1512–20 • Sultan who brought Muslim holy cities of Mecca and Medina under Ottoman control

Shah Jahan (SHAH juh-HAHN), 1592–1666 • Mughal emperor who built Taj Mahal

Sinan (see-NAHN), **Mimar** (mee-MAHR), 1489–1588 • Chief architect of Ottoman sultans

Sobieski (SOH-bee-skee), **Jan,** 1629–96 • King of Poland, saved Vienna from Turkish invasion

Sophia, 1657–1704 • Ruled Russia on behalf of her brothers, continued Westernization of the country

Suleyman (soo-lay-MAHN) **the Magnificent** 1494–1566 • Ottoman sultan at height of empire

Timur (TEE-mer) **the Lame**, also known as **Tamerlane** (TAM-er-lane), 1336– 1405 • Central Asian conqueror

Vytautas (vih-TAO-tuhs), 1350–1430 • Grand duke of Lithuania

Wallenstein, (VAH-luhn-shteen), **Albrecht von,** (ahl-BRECHT), 1583–1634 • Habsburg general during Thirty Years' War

AN AGE OF EMPIRES, 1200–1750

SOME PRONUNCIATIONS

Anatolia (an-uh-TOE-lee-uh)

Baghdad (BAG-dad)

Beijing (bay-jing)

Burkhara (boo-KAHR-ah)

Cape Bojador (BAH-juh-dor)

Damascus (duh-MASS-cus)

Dunhuang (dwun-hwahng)

Goa (GO-uh)

Hangzhou (hahng-jo)

Hispaniola (his-pah-NEE-OH-luh)

Hormuz (or-MOOZ)

Isfahan (ihs-fuh-HAHN)

Karakorum (ka-ruh-KOHR-uhm)

Macao (muh-COW)

Madeira (muh-DEER-uh)

Malacca (meh-LAH-kuh)

Manchuria (man-CHUR-ee-a)

Mecca (MEH-ka)

Medina (meh-DEE-nuh)

Nanjing (nahn-jing)

Ndongo (ehn-DONG-oh)

Novgorod (NOHV-gah-rod)

Samarkand (SA-muhr-kand)

Yangzhou (yahng-jo)

INTRODUCTION

DAYS OF EMPIRE

Imagine being alone on a pristine Caribbean beach or a vast plain in Central Asia and noticing on the far horizon the billowing of a puffy white sail or the dust of tens of thousands of horses coming at you. At first you might be intrigued, then filled with terror. If you were a Taino Indian living in the Caribbean, you would never have seen a ship like Columbus's *Santa Maria* before. If you lived in Samarkand, a city in Uzbekistan, you would know that those thousands of horses probably belonged to the most feared warrior in Asia, Genghis Khan.

Persian warriors were among the many cultures seeking to expand their territory. Such central Asian horsemen swept across vast areas of land and often brutally crushed any resistance as they sought to build their own empires.

The period 1200 to 1750, the time of Isabella of Castile (the Spanish queen who paid for Columbus's journey), Genghis Khan (conqueror of the largest land empire ever), and other rulers, is called the Age of Empires because so many major leaders were fighting to stake their claims and expand their boundaries. Innovations in warfare, from guns to faster sail ships to large cannons, made it possible for some nations to expand. Other empires were built on fast horses and skilled bowmen—and an occasional woman archer. This book is about several of these empires, their rulers, and the changes brought by conquest.

Why would people risk their lives fighting to create an empire, or spend the money it takes to pay armies to build one? According to most dictionaries an empire is a nation or people who claim dominion or power over others. The word comes from the Latin *imperium*, "to rule over." So, why rule over others? One reason, often used to explain the cause of war, is that the nation is threatened; that it has a need for safer boundaries. In Central Asia, where open plains often meant few natural borders, tribes often did have their security threatened. It is not surprising, then, that several of the empires appearing in this book—the Mongol, the Manchu, the Mughal, the Ottoman, and that of Timur the Lame—have Central Asian origins. It was a tough neighborhood, and its people had to learn to fight early in life.

Another reason for empire is that the leaders feel they have something to offer others, a new religion or "civilization" to reduce the enemy's "backwardness." Arabs invaded Spain and Portugal to advance Islam; the Muslim Ottomans tried to do the same in central Europe. Spanish explorers went to look for gold, but also to bring the Catholic religion to the Americas. Some of the worst wars in European history, such as the ones fought by Catholic Habsburgs (an extended royal family) against German Protestants or by a group of crusaders known as the Teutonic Knights against Poland, pitted Christian against Christian.

St. Vincent, patron saint of navigation, holds a caravel, a ship used to explore the coast of Africa, on this 1555 Portuguese coin. Soon after Portugal began extracting gold from mines in southern Africa, the government began minting more important coins using this precious metal instead of silver.

Sometimes neighboring states were just in a mess. Rivalries, civil wars, poor rulers, or natural disasters could make a people vulnerable and open to a takeover by another state. The Manchu, who lived in the northeast of what is now China, sat on the Chinese border watching rebel armies and inept Chinese emperors until the time was right to invade. The Habsburg Empire sometimes stirred up trouble in neighboring Poland or Hungary, hoping to gain control. The conquest of Mexico by the Spanish explorer Cortés would not have been possible without the failure of Moctezuma, the Mexica leader, to gain the loyalty of his conquered subjects.

Underlying the urge to acquire an empire was often the desire to gain wealth, whether it was the gold of the Americas or the wealth of the Silk Road cities in Central Asia. Soldiers grumbled if they did not get their share of looted cities; emperors wanted their cut, too. Occasionally, as for the Portuguese in Africa and the Tartars, a Turkish-speaking group in Russia, their "loot" consisted of human lives sold into slavery. People in the Age of Empires did not invent slavery. But because of the vast distances involved, slaves

> *"In this vast empire there are verily men of every nation under heaven and of every sect; and each and all are allowed to live according to their own sect. For this is their opinion... that every man is saved in his own sect."*
>
> —Andrew of Perugia, Catholic missionary of the Order of Friars Minor, Letter describing Mongolian religious attitudes, 13th century

lacked the ability to escape or return home and were often more vulnerable in strange cultures. Some slaves were luckier than others, like the women in the Ottoman court who held the powerful position of valide sultan, which literally means mother of the sultan, or king. But these were few.

Then, there were some rulers of empires, and Genghis Khan of the Mongols is probably one, who just plain enjoyed the adventure of taking more lands and seeing what was over the horizon. Once started, however, plundering for its own sake was difficult to stop because the army might turn on the ruler. Frequently sons fought fathers; imprisoning or killing a son is a frequent occurrence found in these pages. Transportation lines got long and thinly defended; men and women got tired; and empires, like Timur the Lame's, could collapse more quickly than they expanded.

Once in power, rulers had to decide whether the empire was merely for their glory and fortunes, or whether all should benefit. Should a ruler's values prevail, or did conquered people have rights to their own religion and culture? The rulers from Central Asia generally used the herding model. Conquered peoples were like cows or sheep. They could be "milked" for extra taxes and work, but were allowed to practice their religion to keep them content. Europeans, however, were more likely to expect their subjects to follow their own values, particularly in religion. Generally, rulers of empires, if they wanted to keep power, provided some economic benefits to the people conquered, a "pax" of some kind.

The word *pax* is Latin for peace, and the phrase *Pax Romana* is used to describe the road system and trade that went on throughout the Roman empire. There was also a *Pax Mongolica* of trade along the Silk Road from China to the Mediterranean. Russian advances into Siberia created a trade network from Alaska to the Russian city of St. Petersburg. Although the rulers of empires and the upper classes usually got most of the profits, they often built the palaces, temples, mosques, and churches that form part of our world heritage. However, some ordinary people—merchants, artisans, and farmers—also benefited from these wider markets. People brought new ideas along the roads, and it was often when new ideas suddenly collided with old that some of the most thoughtful philosophies and greatest art and literature appeared.

There were also terrible costs in empires, particularly in the early days of gaining control. It was not just the cities damaged, such as Samarkand or Buda in Hungary or the Syrian city of Damascus or China's northern capital, Beijing. They were rebuilt. It was the lives lost or torn, and the destroyed books we will never read or the ones not written out of fear. Battle casualties are present in this book, but who can understand what 15,000 Hungarian lives lost at their town of Mohacs really means, or the millions of Americans who died of disease because Europeans brought epidemics with them? Empires require imagination.

Though there is plenty of controversy among historians about empires and what they did or did not do, few could deny that empires produced intriguing people. Some, such as emperors Babur of the Mughals, or Kangxi of the Manchu, tell us outright about their lives. Others, like Tsar Ivan the Terrible of Russia, remain mysteries. For some, like Genghis Khan, the individual seems to be the driving force behind the empire. Others, like Prince Henry the Navigator of Portugal and Isabella of Castile, though exceptional individuals, were leading figures in a time of other leaders with similar goals for their states. There are remarkable characters in these pages; some to admire, some to criticize—just like the people in our world.

"In the fog you did not go astray nor did you forsake
me in the battle,
When it was wet, we bore the rain together; when it was
cold, we bore the cold together."

—Genghis Khan, praising his generals,
The Secret History of the Mongols, 13th century

CHAPTER 1

GOLDEN KHAN, GOLDEN REINS, GOLDEN HORDE

THE MONGOLS RIDE OUT

Above all, the Mongols were about movement. A European monk, William of Rubruck, visiting the Mongols in the 14th century, found, "They have no fixed residence and never know where they will be the next day." In ordinary times, they were a nomadic clan of Central Asia, leading their herds of horses, sheep, and cattle from one pasture to another as the weather changed. In the extraordinary times of the 13th century, their leader, Genghis Khan, led them from city to city until they had conquered territory from Korea to central Europe.

Theirs was the largest land empire in history, and Genghis Khan one of the most debated figures. For some, the Mongols were like a hurricane that blasted its way through civilizations. Others see their empire as protecting flourishing trade networks. Almost all historians agree, however, that it took tough horses, tough people, and a tough leader to create an empire that covered almost half the time zones of the world.

These Mongol fighters look relaxed as they rest in camp while their horses graze nearby. The neatly stacked weapons and the orderly arrangement of the men, however, hint at their readiness for battle and their ability to quickly mount attacks.

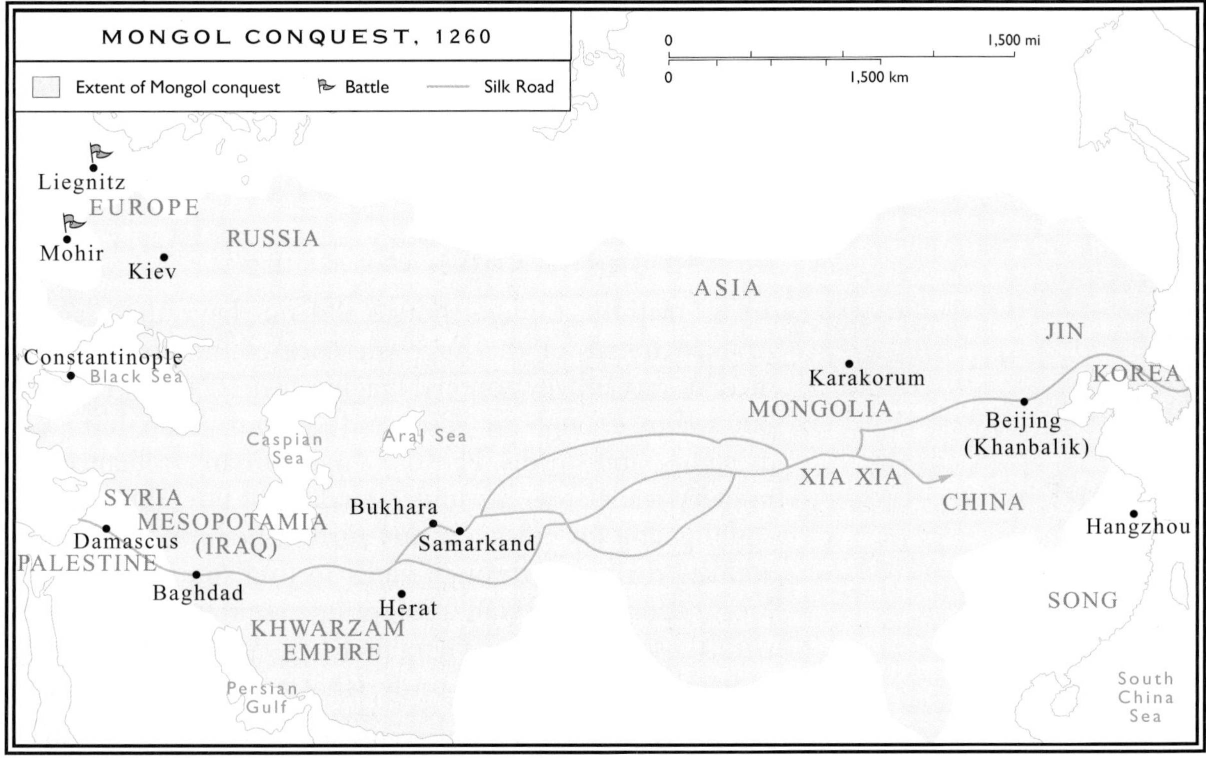

The Mongols relied on horses. They did have sheep to provide wool for clothing and felt for the round tents, or *gers*, they lived in. Cattle, too, provided milk and meat. But horses were at the center of Mongol culture. As one of Genghis Khan's best friends, the Mongol general Bodunchar, said, "If the horse dies, I die; if it lives, I survive." Not only did they rely on horses for transportation and hunting, they also drank mare's milk and curdled it into cubes of soft cheese for eating. Riding across barren lands, riders would sometimes open up a vein in the horse's neck so they could drink the blood, then re-close the vein and go on. Before a journey or battle, a Mongol shaman (religious leader) would sprinkle mare's milk on people for luck, and craftspeople would make army banners from black horses' tails.

The most important Mongol generals were referred to as the Four Geldings, and Mongol control as the Golden Reins. With all this reliance on their animals, it is not surprising that Mongol law said anyone who hit a horse in the eye would be executed. Another European monk who sought out the Mongols in the 13th century, John of Plano Carpini, was amazed: "They have such of number of horses... that I do not believe there are so many in all the rest of the world."

HORSE SENSE AND HARD LIVES

To be truthful, Mongol horses did not have the grace of Arabian horses or the huge presence of European horses, bred to carry heavily armored knights. Instead, they were small but tough enough to withstand Central Asian blizzards, droughts, and storms. Part of Genghis Khan's brilliance as a military leader was his understanding of how these horses could gallop for miles, quickly turn or perform maneuvers, and dig their way through snow to find something to eat. Most nations would wait until spring to start wars, but winter, with these horses, was Genghis Khan's preferred time. The Mongols were even able to do what no one else in history

Mongol horses were small but able to carry the essentials of Mongol warfare: the archer, his strong bow, an assortment of arrows and his food supplies, including curded milk. A Mongol proverb explained this mobile lifestyle: "When a Mongol is separated from his horse, what is there left for him to do but die?"

has done, not Napoleon in 1812, nor Hitler in the 1940s: defeat Russia in the winter.

The Mongol people matched the hardiness of their horses. Both sexes started to ride about the age of three. John of Plano Carpini, used to more limited roles for European women, was startled to find that "Young girls and women ride and gallop on horseback with agility, like men. We even saw them carrying bows and arrows." When Mongols went on military campaigns, women frequently tore down camp, found food, and gathered spent arrows after the battle. These tasks meant they had to keep up with the army. Carpini was also impressed with the length of time Mongols could stay in the saddle. If necessary, they would strap themselves in and, changing horses, could ride 100 miles at a time. They learned at an early age to hunt together, driving wild animals into ever-narrowing circles. Once the animals had enclosed a relatively small area, the person in charge would give a signal to shoot arrows into the prey. To do this maneuvering, to wait for the right time, to follow directions, and to shoot accurately—all these skills were important in military training as well.

Although Genghis Khan never sat for a portrait during his lifetime, his image was often imagined by later artists. Known for his loyalty to his soldiers, Genghis told his bodyguards, "It is my intention that your wives and daughters shall be dressed in gold embroidered dresses, ride quiet geldings, and have clean and pleasant tasting water to drink, [and] your herds shall have good pastures."

Genghis Khan, like his horses and people, was a hard man from a hard background. His real name was Temujin, and it was only in 1206 that he united the Central Asian clans and became the Khan, or leader, with the title of Genghis, which means universal. The 13th century book by an unknown author entitled *The Secret History of the Mongols* tells about his early life and provides two revealing points about him. First of all, he was born with a blood clot in his hand, foreshadowing the bloodshed that would come with his conquests. And from an early age, his people saw "a fire in his eyes and a light in his face." He had drive and intelligence.

He needed both to survive. His father was killed by the Tartars. His mother, Ho'elun, had been a bride kidnapped from another tribe, and the Mongols deserted the widow and her children. They were forced to live on whatever they could find: plants, small animals, or stolen livestock. Half starved, the children became desperate. When a stepbrother took food away from Temujin and his brother, they killed him. Ho'elun was furious. "How can you, older brothers or younger brothers, act like this toward one another? We have no other friends than our own shadows." His mother's intervention then, and again later when she saved another brother from the wrath of Genghis, made him aware that the women in his family often moderated his anger. Though he was married to more than one wife, as was the custom, he respected their views and took at least one on every campaign for advice. Forced to live close to nature, he observed it closely and used it to understand military affairs. As he told his troops, "In daylight watch with the vigilance of an old wolf; at night with the eyes of a raven; and in battle, fall upon the enemy like a falcon."

He also learned how to survive complicated rivalries among clans or tribal groups. Genghis knew from the beginning that he would avenge the death of his father by the Tartars. He had also suffered capture by the Tayichi'ut clan, the kidnapping of his wife Borte by another, the Merkit, and attacks by a third, the Naiman. With the help of his army, and by playing one clan against the other, by 1202 he had virtually wiped out the Tartars and defeated the rest. In 1206, all of the remaining clans met together at a Great Assembly and he was established as the great khan, Genghis Khan.

"On sighting Batu's camp, I was struck with awe. His own dwellings had the appearance of a large city stretching far out lengthways and with inhabitants scattered around in every direction for a distance of three or four leagues [one league equals about 1,500 paces]."

—William of Rubruck, describing his visit to the Golden Horde in Russia, 1253–55

CONQUERING THE WORLD

After Genghis gained control of the Central Asian clans, he decided to take on the rest of Asia. Exactly why he wanted to do so is not clear. Certainly, one way to keep the clans busy and prevent civil war was to encourage their attacks on someone else. A busy army was a loyal army. Then, too, the wealth of China was tempting, and the iron forged there was necessary for weapons. Genghis also seems to have enjoyed fighting. In a debate with friends about the greatest joys in life—family, storytelling, hunting—Genghis Khan gave his view: "Man's greatest good fortune is to chase and defeat his enemy, seize his total possessions, leave his married women weeping and wailing, ride his gelding."

The first attacks went east. China in the thirteenth century was divided into three dynasties, the Xia Xia, the Jin (Chin), and the Song. It took 60 years, with Genghis's grandson Khubilai Khan finishing the work, to defeat all three kingdoms and unify China by 1279. To the west, Genghis and his sons and generals defeated the Khwarazm Empire (around Iran) and then the lands of Syria, Iraq, and Palestine. Driving further north, his son Jochi and his grandson Batu defeated the Russians and forced their princes to accept the Mongols (there called the Golden Horde) as their rulers. Going into Europe in 1241, they defeated the Hungarians at the Battle of Mohir, and the Poles leading a European coalition at Liegnitz, Poland, in 1241, before pulling back. Along the way, they gained a reputation for brutality and invincibility.

Confronted by well-fortified Chinese cities, the Mongols added new tactics to their arsenal. Learning quickly from captured Chinese soldiers, they began to use gunpowder effectively and to dig tunnels under towers to lay explosive mines beneath them.

Though Mongol conquests required a variety of tactics, they had some general ways of operating. They chose their targets well. For example, Samarkand in Uzbekistan and its neighboring city, Bukhara, were important cities on the Silk Road that exchanged Chinese, Middle Eastern, and European goods such as pottery, carpets, furs, glass, and especially silk. Control of Samarkand would give Genghis a stranglehold on trade and taxes. After deciding on a target, the Mongols used their spy system to check out the strengths and weaknesses of their enemies. The Mongols, however, did not start with an attack on Samarkand. The first fighting focused on control of the countryside and other cities near Samarkand. These were the encircling tactics of the hunt. Then the attack could begin. Usually, unless the target was a group that the Mongols

"With one stroke a world which billowed with fertility was laid desolate, and the regions thereof became a desert, with the greater part of the living dead, and their skin and bones crumbling dust, and the mighty were humbled."

—Persian historian Juvaini, lamenting the Mongol destruction of the Persian irrigation system, *The History of the World Conqueror,* 13th century

really hated, like the Tartars, they would give the city warning of the coming fight. If the city surrendered, the citizens would be treated relatively well. The Mongols would take goods and weapons, but the people and their buildings would survive. If the people resisted, the Mongols would show little mercy.

When Samarkand decided to fight back in 1220, the Mongols began moving toward the city's fortress walls, or at least their prisoners did. The city of Bukhara had fallen to them earlier, and the Mongols had taken young men as prisoners to dig tunnels or set up defenses. Now they forced the prisoners toward the gates of Samarkand, making its inhabitants waste their ammunition on their own people. It must have been extremely demoralizing to kill former friends, neighbors, and family members that the Mongols had imprisoned.

Still unable to break through, the Mongols pulled one of their oldest tricks. An old Mongolian proverb said, "Out of any thirty-six stratagems you may devise, by far the best one is to flee." They pretended that they were beaten and pulled back. The people of Samarkand felt so triumphant that they sent their main army out of their fortress to chase the scattering Mongols. Now the Mongols, having lured the defenders out of their protective walls, launched an ambush and wiped out the defenders. It was the classic Mongol "attack-flee-ambush" trick. By this time, the bribed Turkish mercenaries inside the walls, who were originally hired by the people of Samarkand, refused to continue the fight. The people of Samarkand had little choice but to surrender.

Fifty thousand of the inhabitants paid all they had to be saved, skilled workers were sent back to Mongolia, the poor became slaves, and most of the buildings were destroyed. The Turkish troops who had betrayed the defenders thought they would be rewarded. Instead, Genghis had them all executed. He prized loyalty not only in his own men, but also in his enemies. The story of Samarkand, with variations, was repeated throughout the empire as the Mongols conquered the great cities of China, the Middle East, and Europe—the northern and eastern Chinese capitals, Beijing and Hangzhou;

the Iraqi capital, Baghdad; the capital of Syria, Damascus; the Afghani city of Herat; and Kiev, in Ukraine.

It was not just clever tactics that made the Mongol Army so effective. Their composite bow, made from several pieces of wood and strong enough to send arrows 200 yards, was deadly. Their variety of arrows for attacking, signaling, and fire starting made them flexible fighters. For quick mobility, the army was divided into groups of 10 in a squad, and then 10 of these squads made up a larger force. Discipline was hard. If any person let down his group of 10, all would be punished. Along with this discipline, however, went a shared sense of hardship. Batu, Genghis's grandson, who led the Golden Horde in Russia, put it this way: "If we are to die, let us all die... if the time has now come, let us all endure it." Genghis Khan chose his generals wisely, with an eye for talent and loyalty. Two of the best generals in history were Subotei and Jebe, who were with him at Samarkand and who defeated five major civilizations in their careers. There were times when Genghis's sons and generals were at one end of the continent while he was at the other. Yet no general rebelled against him.

Mongol artisans hammered and engraved these silver horse trappings, covered with a thin layer of gold, to resemble lotus blossoms, a sacred flower in China and India. The ornaments were then attached to straps across the horse's chest, sides, and hindquarters.

Though Genghis was an able military commander, his reputation and that of his heirs as world leaders is still controversial. After his death, his empire continued, though increasingly it was split up into sections with different sons and grandsons ruling. The most lasting parts of control exerted by Mongolian descendants were the Golden Horde in Russia and the Yuan dynasty in China

The historians who believe the Mongols and Genghis destroyed civilizations have a good case. At the beginning, Mongols preferred nomadic society. They felt that if cities were destroyed or the fragile irrigation systems of the

Middle East neglected, that merely meant more open land for pasture. The Mongols burned the libraries of Damascus and the church records of Kiev, wiping out much knowledge of the past. Lovely churches in Kiev, beautiful mosques in Baghdad, and serene temples in China and Korea were no more. We do not know the human costs of these wars. Carpini described a scene in Ukraine that was repeated elsewhere: "We came across countless skulls and bones of dead men lying about the ground. Kiev had been a very large and thickly populated town, but now it has been reduced almost to nothing."

What could balance such destruction? Once in power, the Mongols restored international trade that had been interrupted for centuries. Silk Road traffic was rebuilt, from Korea to Kiev. European merchants, such as Niccolo and Marco Polo, found their way back and forth in the China trade. When the Polos reported that paper money was used as a medium of exchange, Europeans scoffed. Who would trust paper instead of real gold or silver? In fact, the Mongols, promising gold and silver later, had made the routes so dependable that paper money could be used. Some of the destruction of the Mongols was balanced by the increase in trade.

Goods were not the only things exchanged in this era. Mongols were tolerant of religious ideas. While their own religion was based on spiritual ties with nature, especially with their important Blue Sky god Tangri, Genghis was curious about other religions and tolerated Christian, Muslim,

Genghis Khan is surrounded by three of his sons, whom he called his four steeds. Although Jochi was the eldest and most capable son, he did not succeed to the throne.

Too Many Sons, Not Enough Empires

“ **ANONYMOUS, THE SECRET OF THE MONGOLS, 13TH CENTURY**

This excerpt from the Secret History of the Mongols *whose author is unknown but scholars suspect may be one of Genghis Khan's adopted brothers, tells the story of the passing of authority from Genghis to one of his sons. No one seemed willing to bring up the topic of what would happen if Genghis were to die until his wife Yisui, herself childless, did so. Genghis Khan's solution of having his most likable son, Ogodei, take over was only temporary. With Ogodei's death, the rivalries and splitting of the empire began.*

Just as he [Genghis] was about to ride out [against the enemy], Lady Yisui petitioned him saying: "My khan, you think to cross high ridges, ford wide rivers, fight distant campaigns and pacify your many nations. But no creature is born immortal. When your body like a withered tree comes crashing down, to whose will you entrust the tangled hemp of your people? When your body, like the stone base of a pillar, crumbles and falls, to whose will you entrust this flock of red-polls, your people? In which of your four steeds, the sons who were born to you, will you put your trust? Your sons, your younger brothers, your people, even my unworthy self, have realized that a choice must be made. The decision is yours." Genghis Khan answered her with a decree[:] "Though she is merely a woman of noble blood, Yisui's words are beyond reproach. It hasn't occurred to any of the rest of you to come forward with such a petition, and, having no precedent to follow forgot myself, having no fear of death, became complacent. Jochi is my eldest son. What do you say?" But before Jochi could utter a word Cha'adai spoke up: "Are you asking Jochi to speak because you intend to name him as your successor? How could we let ourselves be governed by a Merkit foundling?" Then Jochi leapt to his feet and seized Cha'adai's collar. "The khan our father has never said that I was any different from the rest of you," he said. "Why do you discriminate against me?... If you can wrestle me to the ground, I swear I'll never rise again from the place where I fall. Let my father decide the matter!" As Jochi and Cha'adai stood there, holding each other's collars... Genghis Khan listened in silence.

Niccolo and Marco Polo, Venetian merchants, kneel before Khubilai Khan in this European painting. The actual court of the khan was much more elaborate. Of its grandeur, Marco Polo later wrote, "I have not told half of what I saw."

Buddhist, and Hindu beliefs. In the capital city the Mongols began to build at Karakorum, in what is now central Mongolia, there were twelve temples of various sects, two Muslim mosques, and one church. When asked about this diversity of belief, Genghis said, "Even as God has given several fingers in the hand, so has He given man several ways."

There was also in Mongol society a certain rough sense of equality, or at least shared experience. Mongol custom encouraged people to give one of every 100 sheep to charity. "Orphan grants" of goods taken in raids were given to children whose fathers had been killed. Women had leadership roles. If a khan died and he and his wife had only young sons, the widow ruled until the next gathering of the clans and the election of a new khan.

The Mongols, when Genghis started out, did not have a written language; that was for their allies to provide for them. Ironically, they conquered some of the most literate societies of the day: the Chinese, Persian, and Arabic. In fact, much of their history was written by their enemies. Genghis Khan was not concerned with hiring court historians to write about him, nor in building huge monuments to his memory. When he died in 1227, still on a military campaign, soldiers brought his body back to Mongolia and hid it in the mountains, where it remains undiscovered. Horses were used to trample all traces of loose earth, concealing his grave.

CHAPTER 2

WHO'S NEXT?

THE MONGOLS REACH THEIR LIMIT

What were the Mongols up to now? In early winter of 1241, they destroyed some Hungarian villages and drove the half-starved refugees to the west side of the Danube River. Earlier in the year, the Mongols had captured herds of cattle and left them to graze on the east side of the river. The nearly famished Hungarians could see the cattle just across the water and anxiously waited for the river to freeze. Several men made attempts to reach the cattle to provide food for their weakening families. But the thin ice cracked, and the men were swept away by the icy water. Finally, the ice was thick enough to cross and some of the refugees could, at last, find food to survive. For the Mongols, they now knew their troops could safely cross the river—without their own testing and loss of life. Who were these people with such schemes?

The appearance of the Mongols, seemingly out of nowhere, forced a rethinking of religious beliefs. How could such a violent people as the Mongols represent the will of heaven? The first reaction to the Mongols was usually one of disdain. The bishop of Winchester in England saw them as infidels (non-Christians) fighting more infidels. "Let these dogs destroy one another," he wrote his king, Henry III. The Chinese also looked down on the nomadic Mongols as uncivilized. Arabs, too disliked the Mongols; they might fight Christians over the Holy Land, but at least Christians shared their Biblical heritage. Muslims thought the Mongols, with

In this painting, Genghis Khan assaults the Indian city of Tangut with an overwhelming number of soldiers and weapons. Although the Mongols collected great wealth, the hot and humid Indian climate wore down the Mongol horses and made for limp bowstrings, forcing the attackers to pull back.

Dinner Fit for a King

MARCO POLO, THE TRAVELS OF MARCO POLO, 13TH CENTURY

The Venetian traveler Marco Polo offered this description of the Chinese court in his account, The Travels of Marco Polo. *Having spent 17 years in China beginning in 1275, Polo didn't think to write about his experiences until he was a prisoner in Venice's rival city of Genoa. Readers were skeptical of some of his claims. Paper money sounded far-fetched, and so did black rocks (coal) that burned. Still, the wealth of Khubilai Khan's court that he described lured others to the great Silk Road trade with China.*

When his Majesty holds a grand and public court... the tables are arranged in such a manner that the Great Khan, sitting on his elevated throne, can overlook the whole.... The greater part of the officers, and even of the nobles... eat, sitting upon carpets, in the halls; and on the outside stand a great multitude of persons who come from different countries and bring with them many rare curiosities.

In the middle of the hall, where the Great Khan sits at table, there is a magnificent piece of furniture, made in the form of a square coffer, each side of which is... exquisitely carved in figures of animals and gilt. It is hollow within for the purpose of receiving a capacious vase, of pure gold, calculated to hold many gallons.... Within this buffet are also cups or flagons belonging to his Majesty....

The numerous persons who attend... his Majesty and serve him with victuals [food] and drink, are all obliged to cover their noses and mouths with handsome veils or cloths of worked silk, in order that his victuals or his wine may not be affected by their breath. When drink is called for by him, and the page in waiting presented it, he retires three paces and kneels down, upon which the courtiers, and all who are present, in like manner make their prostration. At the same moment all the musical instruments, of which theirs is a numerous band, begin to play and continue to do so until he has ceased drinking, when all the company recover their posture.... It is unnecessary to say anything of the victuals, because it may well be imagined that their abundance is excessive.

their many gods of nature, were truly dangerous and heretical. Yet the Mongols advanced and people had to readjust not only their societies, but their thinking, too, as they wondered why the will of heaven was making these nomads so successful.

ASSASSINS, BRIDES, AND THE TARTAR YOKE

One of the ways of dealing with the Mongols was, as with the old proverb, "If you can't beat them, join them." The Uighur tribe of Turkistan joined the Mongols early, when their clan leader married Genghis Khan's daughter. Since the Mongols had no written language and were unfamiliar with governing cities, the Uighurs became administrators and record keepers. The tribes in southern Russia at first fought the Mongols hard, but once defeated, they joined with them so closely that Westerners lumped them together as "Tartars."

Other societies held out as long as they could and then became very reluctant allies of the Mongols. One of these groups was the Assassins, or Ismailis, located in northern Iran. The term *assassin* comes from this group, an offshoot of the Shi'a branch of the Islamic religion that believes members of the prophet Muhammad's family should lead Islam. Though the Assassins hated Christians, their primary targets for killing were their rivals, Sunni Muslim leaders. They even attacked Saladin, the Muslim hero who had saved Jerusalem from attack by the crusader Richard the Lionhearted in 1192.

The Assassins put members of their group secretly into their enemies' households, and then, on signal, killed their victims. When the Mongol khan heard the report that 400 Assassins were sent to kill him, he quickly attacked. The Mongols used force and deception to oust the Assassins from their strong mountain

Mongol troops guard an upper-class woman as she crosses a river. Mongols often forced their defeated rivals to marry Mongol women, who had a reputation for being strong willed and loyal to the khans.

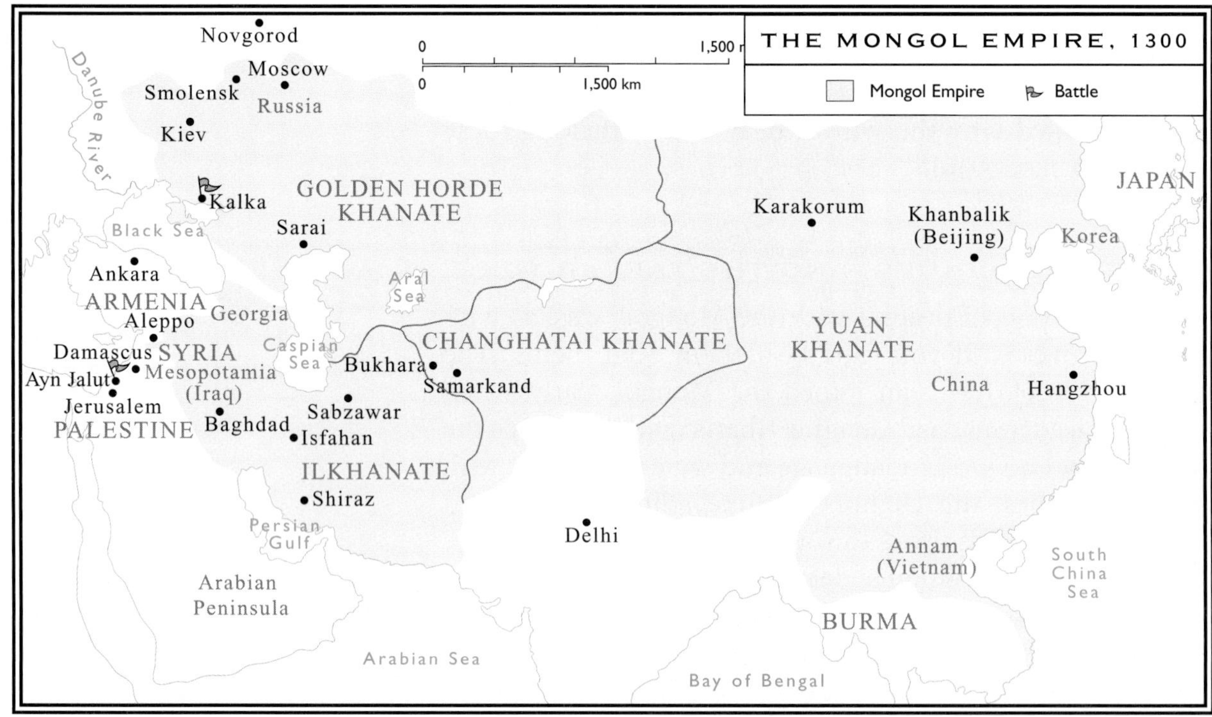

Following the death of Genghis Khan in 1227, the Mongol Empire was divided into four large parts called khanates, each ruled by one of his descendants. Timur the Lame's empire later grew out of the region occupied by the Changhatai Khanate, but by the start of the 16th century, all four khanates had disappeared.

forts. The Assassins expected to join the Mongol Army as promised by the Khan and delighted in their good treatment. Instead, the Mongols killed their leaders and dismantled their remaining defenses. There was little grief at their demise. As one Muslim historian, Juvayni, wrote, "So was the world cleansed which had been polluted by their evil."

Korea also tried to resist the Mongols, then accommodated, but with much different results. The Mongols saw Korea as a nation that could furnish rice, soldiers, and the naval power they lacked. Mongol attacks on Korea began in 1231, and eventually the Mongols defeated Korea. By 1254, the Mongols controlled Korean affairs, making the crown princes marry Mongols, using the Korean Navy, and putting heavy tax burdens on the people. One of the most hated of these burdens was the yearly "tax" of 1,000 young women to be sent to China to marry soldiers in the Mongol Army. At first, the Koreans tried to send criminals, homeless women, or poor widows. But Cheguktaejang, a great-granddaughter of Genghis Khan who was married to a Korean king, saw through this ruse. One Korean official shaved his daughter's head so she appeared too ugly to be taken. Seeing this, Cheguktaejang grew so angry that she had the father tortured, the family's property taken, and the young girl beaten with metal chains and forced into marriage. This tax lasted for almost a century.

Russia, too, saw heavy burdens. A folk song of the time said, "If a man has no money, they took his child. If he had no child, they took his wife. If he had no wife, he himself was taken." After losing a battle at Kalka, now Ukraine, in 1223, the Russians submitted to what they called the Tartar Yoke. One of Russia's heroes, Alexander Nevskii, had protected the Russian city of Novgorod from attacks from the Swedes and the Teutonic Knights, Catholic crusaders from northern Germany. Even he had to deal with the Mongols and work with them. The leader of the Golden Horde, Batu, sent Nevskii a letter, in which he said: "You know that God has subjected to me many peoples. Do you alone wish not to submit yourself to me?" Some in Novgorod wanted to fight further, but Nevskii went to Batu and submitted. Russian princes who worked with the Mongols were rewarded with a *yarlik,* a slice of the tax collection money. Prince Fedor Rostislavovich of Smolensk did even better. He married into Batu's family and received 36 cities to control. For more than 200 years, the Golden Horde controlled Russia until the princes of Moscow grew strong enough to challenge them.

Still other conquered nations, convinced of their own superiority even though the Mongols had defeated them, waited until they were absorbed into the Mongol culture before slowly reintroducing their former customs and

"It is better to be at the right place with one hundred men than to be somewhere else with ten thousand."

—Timur the Lame, advice about moving troops, late 1390s

In Chinese art, bamboo trees growing from rocks often symbolized the idea of strength (bamboo) persisting in the face of hardship (rocks). During the Yuan dynasty, when the Mongols controlled China, artists, such as Li Khan, used bamboo to represent Chinese resistance.

restoring their civilizations. One of these societies was China. The Mongols tried to destroy some Chinese institutions. One of these was the examination system, based on the philosopher Confucius's belief that highly educated men who could pass difficult tests should administer the government. Mongols, on the other hand, prized military leadership. With the examinations ended, scholars and artists turned to writing plays and operas and making paintings, all of which often criticized the Mongol system with seeming innocence. A plum blossom in the snow, for example represented a flowering amidst hard Mongol times. Bamboo in a design showed the importance of bending but not breaking.

A NOMADIC ARMY LOSES ITS GRIP

Dealing with such a complicated society as in China, Mongols in power began to change. An adviser to Ogodei, one of Genghis's sons who ruled in China, told him that an empire might be conquered, but not be ruled, on horseback. They needed Chinese administrators. The Mongols took a Chinese name, Yuan (Original) for their dynasty, ordered records to be kept in Chinese, and mixed old court ceremonies with Mongolian customs. Though Khubilai Khan kept a portion of his elaborate gardens planted in steppe grasses and had huge stables, each generation of Mongols spent less time on the steppe and intermarried with the people they had conquered. By 1315, the Mongols even brought back the examination system.

There were some peoples, however, who managed to escape defeat even though the Mongols attacked them. Europe had some terrible times, with Hungary overrun and eastern Europe subject to conquest. When the 19th-century novelist Bram Stoker made his vampire character, Dracula, a descendent of Genghis Khan, he was demonstrating how long the Mongols lingered in the European imagination.

The Europeans, however, got lucky. In 1241, Ogodei, the son who succeeded Genghis, died. The Mongol leaders turned back from attacks and rode to Mongolia to select the next khan. Though Russia remained under Mongol rule, large invasions into the rest of Europe stopped. Perhaps the lack of wide pastures or the difficulty in fighting in more wooded areas also saved Europe from more conquest. Japan, too, escaped conquest when large storms destroyed two separate invasion attempts by the Mongol fleet.

"Now I have heard that the imperial court intends to make Korea into a Yuan province by establishing a provincial government there. . . . Now for no reason, Korea, a small country that has existed for more than four hundred years, will be extinguished one morning."

—Korean writer Yi Chehyon, letter to Yuan emperor protesting plan to destroy Korean independence, 14th century

The Mongols did not have much luck holding on after their initially successful attacks on Annan (Vietnam), Burma, and Java. The Mamluks of Egypt caused them the greatest difficulties, however. Usually the Mongols checked out their enemies pretty well, but they assumed that the Mamluk leader was just another local dignitary with little military experience. Instead, the Mamluks created an army by buying young Turkish boys as slaves. They were raised in barracks and taught to fight, ride, and practice military strategy. Eventually, the Mamluks became so powerful that they controlled Egypt. At the Battle of Ayn Jalut in 1260, the Mamluks defeated a portion of the Mongol forces. The battle proved that the Mongols were not unbeatable, and the

In this dramatic 19th-century painting, Japanese sailors summon a kamikaze, or divine wind, to defeat the combined Mongol, Chinese, and Korean fleet that attacked Japan in the 13th century. A fierce storm devastated the attackers, protecting Japan from foreign invasion.

A Mongol saddle adorned with gold demonstrates how warriors, who lacked permanent residences, might show off their accumulated wealth. The width of the saddle enabled the archer to shift from side to side when firing his bow.

Mamluks began their conquest of Syria and Palestine, replacing the Mongols.

With the decline of Mongol power in the Middle East, other men tried to imitate Genghis Khan's successful conquests. The man who came closest to doing so was Timur, who came from the area around Samarkand. He is better known in history as Tamerlane, or Timur the Lame because he was badly wounded in battle and limped. Though he came from a Turkish tribe and was born about 1330, a century after Genghis Khan's victories, he tried to link himself with the Mongol ruler. He married one of Genghis's descendants, Saray Mulk, who became one of his closest advisers. He used another descendent of Genghis as a puppet to pretend that the Mongol royal family still ruled. Timur did have many qualities of Genghis. He was a good strategist, a skilled fighter, and had personal drive built on childhood hardship.

"Slung from saddles,
skulls jangle together,
crying.
There are officers whose
backs bear eighty
wounds;
Torn flags envelop the
corpses lying at the side
of the road.
The survivors, resigned to
dying, mourn the fall of
the citadel that now lies
empty;
In the victory bulletins,
there will be one name
only, that of the general."

—Chinese poet Zhao Mengfu, describing the Song dynasty's defeat, 1270s

Still, there were differences. Timur, a Muslim, had little religious tolerance, destroying, for example, the Christian kingdom in Georgia between the Black Sea and the Caspian Sea. His attacks against other religions, particularly on the Hindus in Delhi, were merciless. The Mongols had used terror tactics to subdue populations, partly because there were so few Mongols compared to their enemies. After they subdued their enemies, the Mongols were generally content to take as much as they could tax, without causing more destruction. Timur's violence was more intense. He became known for the tower of skulls stacked outside each devastated city he conquered—Aleppo and Damascus (in Syria), Delhi (in India), and Baghdad (in Iraq). Many of these were Muslim cities. After taking the Iranian city of Isfhan, he ordered each of his 70,000 soldiers to bring heads for the pile. Even some of his soldiers balked at killing unarmed civilians, but other soldiers with less conscience did it for them—at a price. At the city of Sabzawaz, according to a history of the Ghurs people who lived in the area that is now part of Iran, Timur had 2,000 living people put into wet plaster to harden and form a tower as the plaster dried and people died. Even in the rough and tumble world of the Middle East at that time, Timur's violence was extreme.

It was also successful. Timur's empire stretched throughout Iran, Iraq, Georgia, Armenia, parts of India, and Russia. He defeated major powers such as the Golden Horde, destroying its capital at Sarai. He defeated the Ottomans, who would later control a major empire of their own, in Turkey at the Battle of Ankara. It was while Timur was making his plans to attack China, trying to match Genghis's empire, that he died in 1405. His heirs, fighting between themselves, ended that dream.

A contemporary Arab historian wrote of Timur the Lame, "He destroyed right custom and went forth wicked with insolent swords [that] destroyed kings and all the noble and learned." Here Timur watches as his soldiers construct a tower of skulls collected from the defeated citizens of Baghdad.

Considering how much Timur destroyed with his armies, it is ironic that he is also known for his support of painters and architects to adorn his cities and court. Samarkand was his capital, and it became a blue-tiled marvel of mosques, schools, and tombs. When the Persian poet Hafiz praised his own city of Shiraz over Samarkand and Bukhara (another city in Uzbekistan) in a poem, he was called into Timur's angry presence. Timur said to him, "How dare you fling at the feet of Shiraz . . . the two cities [Samarkand and Bukhara] which after years of effort, I conquered with the might of my sword, made beautiful by the labors of the best artists and uplifted above all cities in the world?"

Hafiz replied, "It was the same spendthrift tendency . . . which brought me to this place," meaning he acted without thinking. Luckily, Timur had a sense of humor, laughed, and released the poet.

For some, the fierce reign of Timur and the disruption caused by quarreling rulers that followed actually made the Mongol days seem better ones, more stable in trade and religious tolerance. For others, including the Russians, Koreans, and Chinese, Mongol victories pushed them into creating stronger central governments able to withstand attacks. By the middle of the 13th century, some Mongols sensed that change was coming to their people, too. A story about Khubilai Khan and his wife Chabi illustrates this suspicion. When all the treasures, gold, silver, and jade from the defeated Song dynasty were laid out before them, the Mongol officials were delighted. Not Chabi, who turned to her husband in tears. "It has come to my mind at this moment that the Empire of the Mongols also will finish this way," she said. Ming forces overthrew the Yuan dynasty of the Mongols in 1368.

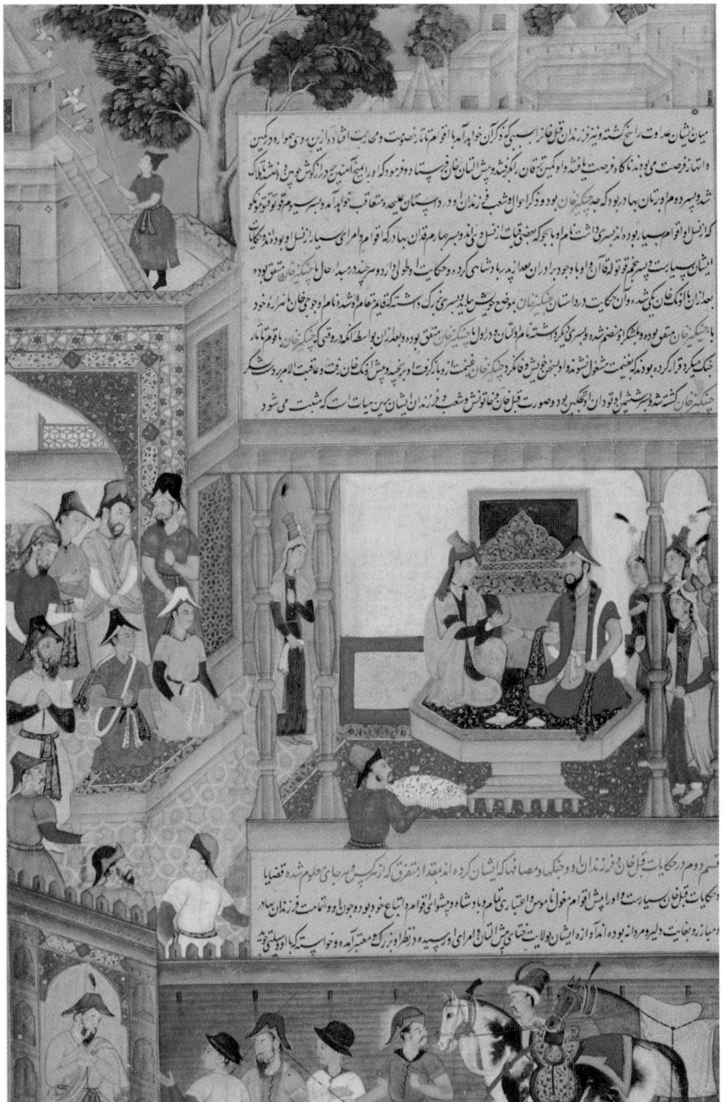

Khubilai Khan and his second wife, Chabi, hold an audience in the royal court. Chabi took an active role in politics, even opposing the Mongol policy of turning fertile agricultural lands into pastures. She told a Chinese adviser to speak up about the issue: "You Chinese are intelligent... When you speak the emperor listens. Why have you not remonstrated with him?"

CHAPTER 3

TWICE AS POWERFUL

POLAND AND LITHUANIA UNITE

Every day at noon, a trumpeter climbs to one of the towers of the Basilica of the Holy Virgin Mary in Krakow, Poland. He blows the melody of the Heynat, the hymn to Mary, out of each of the four windows of the tower. At the fourth window, the trumpeter suddenly breaks off the song. Tourists gathered below may wonder why the trumpeter quits so abruptly, but the people of Krakow know his intent. It reminds them of the bravery of the trumpeter who, unconcerned with his own safety in 1241, warned the city of the approach of the Mongols and who was shot by an arrow in mid-song. The Mongols devastated Krakow in that attack, and again in other invasions.

Yet when the Mongols pulled back to elect a new khan after the death of one of Genghis's sons, they did not return in force to Poland. Some of Genghis Khan's troops did, however, remain in neighboring Russia and, united with other Central Asian groups, became known to the Poles and Lithuanians as the Tartars. In Krakow, on certain festival days, a mock Tartar rides through the streets of the town on a hobbyhorse to make fun of today what was so fearful in the past.

A musician blows trumpet signals from the window of the Basilica of the Holy Virgin Mary in Krakow, Poland. He continues a centuries-old tradition that once warned inhabitants of fires and invading Mongols.

The Tartars were not the only enemy Poland and Lithuania had to face. Without clear geographic borders or mountains and seas to protect them, they had to fight for their land. Poland and Lithuania are separate nations today, just as they were in early history. For more than 500 years, however, their fates were joined together. During the 1400s and 1500s, they united to create the largest European empire, going from the Black Sea to the Baltic Sea, from Ukraine to Prussia, once a part of Germany.

The Poles and Lithuanians chose leaders through a clan system. Candidates had to prove their skills in battle to warriors who would elect leaders by showing up to vote for them. Although sons often inherited their fathers' lands, Polish kings did not inherit the throne, but instead were elected by the *szlachta,* or gentry, a group of relatively well-off individuals who were pledged to fight at their leader's call.

FIGHTING CHRISTIANS AND PIOUS PAGANS

In the early 1300s, Poland and Lithuania looked at each other as unlikely partners. Poland had become Christian in 966 and was drawing closer to western Europe with royal marriages into the French, German, and Scandinavian ruling families. Lithuania, on the other hand, was not a Christian country. The Lithuanian religion included a male sky god, Perkunas, and a female forest god, Madeina. Rather than having churches, Lithuanians met in sacred oak groves where male and female priests tended a fire constantly in respect for the gods. Horses were important symbols. Two

POLAND AND LITHUANIA, 1500–1582

horses carved above the door of a house were there for good luck; it was bad luck was to ride a white horse, which should be reserved for the gods.

Despite their religious differences, the Poles and Lithuanians began to see themselves as allies. They had fought each other over control of the Baltic trade, with its rich fur, amber, salt, and timber traveling from Russia to western Europe. But in the 1300s, they had common enemies: in the south, the Tartars and, in the north, the Teutonic Knights, Catholic crusaders who were mainly German. Having largely escaped the Black Death, the plague that so devastated most of Europe in the 14th century, their populations grew.

The Tartars and the Teutonic Knights saw this growth as a threat and decided it was time to take over Poland and Lithuania before they expanded further. The Teutonic Knights are one of the most controversial subjects in European history. Were they pious, noble Christians, or some of history's most cold-blooded killers? A Knight described one raid: "We set fire and destroyed everything; we killed all what was of masculine sex, captured all the women and children... [as slaves]." The Lithuanians, who, as non-Christians, were one of the Knights' primary targets, wondered why they sent so few priests and built so few churches while sending so many warriors. Because of these German intrusions, the Lithuanians began to include a new prayer in funeral ceremonies, "Go, poor sufferer, into that other happier life, where the Germans will slave for you and not you for the Germans."

To combat the growing power of the Teutonic Knights, the Poles and Lithuanians decided to unite through royal marriages. One of the brides was Anna, a Lithuanian woman who converted to Christianity to marry the Polish king Casimir the Great in the mid-14th century. Popular because of her generosity to the poor, Anna was still suspect to some Poles. A Polish historian writing a 100 years later, thought she was still too pagan for preferring celebration to quiet piety. She liked games, dancing, and, when riding in a coach, "the Queen had to have drums, harps, viols and various other musical instruments playing for her."

"My Knights, see what an ugly thing is pride; for he who yesterday claimed to be master of many a country and kingdom... now lies beyond help, killed in the most wretched manner, proof that pride is worse than modesty."

—Polish chronicler Jan Dlugosz, quoting King Jogaila about the slain Grand Master of the Teutonic Knights, 1455

The huge brick fortress of Malbork, or Marienburg, on the Nogat River in Poland was the headquarters of the Teutonic Knights and actually contains three castles within its walls. Originally founded to help crusaders in the Holy Land, the Knights later attacked Russia, Poland, and Lithuania to gain control of the Baltic area.

Another marriage occurred in 1386 amid much controversy. Neither the bridegroom, Jogaila of Lithuania, nor the bride, Jadwiga of Poland, was enthusiastic about the wedding. Jadwiga had been engaged to an Austrian prince she really liked, but her advisers wanted her to marry a Lithuanian who, the Austrians told her, was pagan, ugly, hairy, and deformed. When her Austrian prince came to stop the marriage, her Polish advisers locked her up. Though she pleaded with her servants for an axe to break down the door to escape to him, she remained locked in until he left. The Poles, desperate to have the Lithuanian marriage, finally let her send two of her trusted knights to see Jogaila and go to the bathhouse with him. Just how ugly was he? The knights reported back that he seemed normal and good-looking enough to them. The Roman Catholic bishop also encouraged the marriage, reminding Jadwiga of her Christian duty to help change pagan Lithuania. Only 12 years old, Jadwiga gave in and agreed to the marriage.

From most reports, it was not a happy one. She spent most of her time with church activities, and he with military affairs and hunting. Even when he tried to cheer her, the attempts failed. After one of Jadwiga's miscarriages, Jogaila wrote her, encouraging her to decorate their rooms in gold and red to make them so cheerful that a baby might come. Jadwiga wrote back that only pious humility and prayer could bring them children. Jadwiga died in childbirth at 25, and her baby died as well.

If the marriage was a mismatch for the two people involved, it was a success politically. Jadwiga encouraged church building and sold her jewels to revive the University of Krakow. Together with Jogaila, she went to Lithuania to encourage people to convert to Christianity. Instead of the sword, she brought white woolen shirts to give to the newly baptized people as symbols of their new lives. The sacred oak groves of the old religion were chopped down, and the fires to the old gods extinguished. Some Lithuanians felt the cutting of the old oak groves was particularly hard to watch, and many of them still mixed old beliefs with new. Even Grand Duke Vytautas of Lithuania, who had converted even before Jogaila, remarked as he rode through some remaining oaks, "The gods once inhabited these woods."

Perhaps the most significant part of Jadwiga and Jogaila's marriage was that their combined forces defeated the Teutonic Knights in one of the most important battles of European history. This battle, on July 19, 1410, is known to Germans as the Battle of Tannenberg, and to the Poles as the Battle of Grunwald. The Teutonic Knights invaded Polish territory, trying to defeat them before their alliance with Lithuania became too powerful. Jogaila formed an unusual alliance against the Knights, getting Tartar troops, who needed the Poles to protect them from Mongols, from southern Russia to support him.

The Teutonic Knights had fewer troops, about 20,000 compared with the allied army of 30,000 to 40,000. Still the Knights had been fighting together for a long time, and had tighter discipline and better equipment. The Knights were overconfident. Going into battle, they would sing the hymn "Christ Is Risen," and their thundering cavalry charges alone could make the enemy run. At Grunwald, the Poles and Lithuanians waited throughout the day, delaying the time of battle. The grand master of the Knights sent them

"As I understand it, God does not punish Poland for nothing.
But chiefly for the harsh oppression visited on the serfs,
For God's sake, have you Poles lost your minds completely?
Your whole welfare, your supply of food, the wealth you amass,
All derives from your serfs. It is their hands which feed you."

—Poet Krzysztof Opalinski, *Satyry of Satires*, 1650

"I began to be annoyed that the movement of the world machine, created for our sake by the best and most systematic Artisan of all [God] were not understood with greater certainty by philosophers, who otherwise examined so precisely the most insignificant trifles of this world."

—Nicolaus Copernicus, criticizing philosophers for not using mathematics, *On the Revolution of the Heavenly Spheres*, 1543

two swords, one for Jogaila and one for Vytautas, taunting the Poles by saying that if they did not have enough equipment to fight, the Knights would furnish it. Insulted, the common soldiers clamored for an attack. Jogaila held them back, stalling the battle until late in the day, when the sun had baked the Knights in their armor, increased their thirst, and tired their horses.

Jogaila and Vytautas had learned a great deal about Central Asian fighting styles from fighting the Tartars. Following the Genghis Khan model, Jogaila surveyed the battle from a rise in the landscape where he could direct his forces. After the battle, his voice was so worn down by shouting orders that, for days afterward, he could barely speak. Vytautas rode into the midst of the battle as a fighting general. When there was a break in the allied lines, Vytautas organized the old Mongol "attack-flee-ambush" tactic to counterattack the Knights charging through the lines.

During the battle, the leadership of the Teutonic Knights was almost completely wiped out. The chronicler of the Knights, Positge, could comment only that "The number of the slain was beyond numbering. May God have pity on them." The Knights had brought with them casks of wine to celebrate their intended victory. Jogaila, fearing the affect of alcohol on his troops, had the casks broken. According to the chronicler Dlugosz, whose father was there, this sent "the wine spilling over heaps of dead bodies and, flowing on mixed with the blood of men and horses, into a red stream which cut itself into a channel through the meadow that leads to the village of Tannenberg."

FLOWERS BEFORE THE FLOOD

In the 15th and 16th centuries, Poland joined with much of western Europe in the Renaissance, a revival of classical Greek and Roman art, literature, and architecture. Although several Poles had international reputations at the time, the most influential figure of the Polish Renaissance is the astronomer Nicolaus Copernicus. His main work, *On the Revolution of the Heavenly Spheres*, published in 1543,

Copernicus's fears that the Catholic Church might ban his book, On the Revolution of the Heavenly Spheres, *which challenged the notion that earth was the center of the universe, came true when it was placed on the Index of Forbidden Books in 1616.*

changed Europeans' perception of the universe and themselves. Before Copernicus, the general view was that the sun and the other planets circled the earth, which was at the center of the universe. His finding that the sun was the center of the solar system clashed with prevailing views, and church officials placed his text on the index of books forbidden to Catholics.

One of the reasons Copernicus could feel relatively free to pursue his interests in science is that Poland in the 15th and 16th centuries was a remarkably tolerant place. In 1264, a prince of Krakow had granted a "General Charter of Jewish Liberties," and later rulers had encouraged Jewish migration

Vote Early and Armored

GUILLAUME LE VASSEUR BEAUPLAN, A DESCRIPTION OF UKRAINE, 1744

Guillaume Le Vasseur Beauplan, a French engineer hired by the Commonwealth of Poland and Lithuania to build forts, published a book about his experiences. The following is his description of how a king was elected in Poland. Beauplan was not actually present, but the election he describes is probably that of John Casimir in 1648.

[The election of the king] is generally held in [an] open field half a league from Warsaw... [in a] small inclosure... about 1000 or 1200 paces in compass, enclosed by a pitiful ditch about five or six foot wide, which serves only to hinder horses from going into the said inclosure; [inside] there are two great tents, one for the election where all the Senators sit and the other where all the Deputies of Provinces met who confer together before they go into the Great Audience of the Senate.... They meet thus every day..., during this time they pose all they can think on toward preserving their liberties.... During the election of the late King Valdislaws, there were no less than 80,000 horses about that little inclosure, all soldiers following the Senators, for every one of them had a little army....

Everyone is attended by his friends and subjects... with a resolution to fight in case they cannot agree. Observe, that all the nobility of the country was upon its guard, every one with his foot in the stirrup ready to mount upon the least disagreement or falling out, to fall on those that should attempt to infringe their liberties. At length, after several sittings and audiences, they agreed upon a Prince for their King; every one or at least the chief of the Senators and Deputies, put his hand to it.... Then everyone, returning to Quarters, gives orders to his troops to be ready to draw up according to the Great General's command, under the great Standard [flag] of the Crown and were ready to cry, "Long live the King" calling him by his name.... Next day they conducted him to St. John's Church at Warsaw where before the Altar the King took his Oath.

to Poland. Tolerance also extended to Protestants, such as the followers of Jan Hus, a church reformer from nearby Bohemia. When Catholic officials from Rome tried to put pressure on King Zygmunt to arrest Protestants as heretics or dissenters, he refused. "Permit me to rule over the goats as well as the sheep," he said.

This attitude of tolerance and openness carried over into political life as well. By 1569, the Polish and Lithuanian Commonwealth had developed three major institutions: the monarchy, a senate, and a legislature elected by the gentry and the cities' leaders. Rather than inheriting the throne as in some other nations, the monarch was voted into power, and new rulers had to promise to protect the rights of the people. In Lithuania in 1529, the local assembly passed a measure remarkable for its time that gave women legal equality with men in owning property and in deciding their own religious beliefs, even if they differed from those of their husbands.

The Renaissance showed promise for Poland and Lithuania as major European nations in the future. Large expanses of land and an openness of ideas were encouraging. Instead, one disaster after another occurred for the commonwealth in the 17th and 18th centuries. Polish historians refer to this period of decline as the Deluge, a storm that is so quick and severe that it overwhelms everything in its path.

The troubles began with the Great Northern Wars of 1558–1721, during which Sweden challenged Poland and Lithuania for control of the Baltic and its rich

"You and I, most honorable Prince, have reached an age when death is near and it behooves us to spend the rest of our time in peace. Let the earth swallow the blood shed in battle between us. Let the wind sweep away the... insults we have exchanged. Let fire purge our anger and madness, and let water wash away the traces of the fires we have started in each other's country."

—Tartar leader Ediga, proposed truce to Vytautas, grand duke of Lithuania, 1419

The Radziwills were the largest landowners in the Commonwealth of Poland and Lithuania, and this artistic, puffed style of costume armor was fitting for the most powerful noble family.

In this romanticized 19th-century artist's conception of the epic 1683 battle, Jan Sobieski, the king of Poland, rides out to defend Vienna against the Ottomans. Though Polish, Sobieski came to the aid of the Habsburg capital because he feared Vienna's fall would lead to Turkish control of central Europe.

trade. Most of the fighting was done on Polish soil, devastating the economy. The continued invasions hurt the small landowners. Large landowners were able to take over what poor farmers could no longer defend or afford to pay taxes on. By the 1770s, more than 50 percent of the land was held by large landholders, called magnates. Stanislaw Slaszic, a Polish author of the time, wrote "The magnates made two nations out of one country," theirs and the rest of Poland. Meanwhile, the neighboring countries (Austria, Russia, and Prussia) were modernizing their armies. Gaining power, they were able to bribe voters in the election of Polish kings.

Even with all these problems, the Polish-led forces of King Jan Sobieski provided one of the finest hours for Poland when they defeated the Ottoman Turks who attacked Vienna. On September 12, 1683, he ordered an advance straight at the tent of the Ottoman general. The surprise strike, pushing through the silken tents, successfully disrupted Ottoman leadership. Sobieski sent a message to the pope, "Veni, vidi, Deus vinxit" ("I came, I saw, God conquered").

The costs of victory, however, were largely borne by Poland. The Poles received no special money, lands, or even long-lasting gratitude. Sobieski, though the elected king, found the magnates even more jealous because of his new international reputation. When Sobieski was old, a bishop urged him to make out his will and state his wishes for a future Poland. He wrote back: "They [the magnates] didn't want to listen to me when I'm alive so why should they obey my wishes when I'm dead?"

By the 18th century, Poland and Lithuania were drifting apart, and their stronger neighbors began taking territory from them. In 1772, Russia, Prussia, and Austria made the First Partition, each taking a part of the commonwealth. In 1793 and 1795 there were two more partitions that erased Poland and Lithuania from the European map as independent nations.

The Poles and Lithuanians did not forget their past. Before he was killed in a revolt against the Russians in 1794, the Polish poet Bruno Jasinski wrote:

> Pay no heed that you are bound by heavy chains,
> Whenever people have said 'I want to be free' they
> have always become free!"

Poland and Lithuania are now independent nations.

After successfully resisting five Swedish sieges between 1655 and 1705, Polish defenders of Czestochowa believed it was this icon of the Virgin Mary and baby Jesus, blackened by the smoke of war, that had saved them. The Black Madonna remains a symbol of Polish independence.

CHAPTER 4

TROUBLED TIMES, TROUBLED TSARS

THE RUSSIAN EMPIRE

The icons of Russia have sad eyes. Even the angels in the painter Andrei Rukyov's *Trinity* seem near tears. Icons, or religious paintings on wood, were meant to bring observers to a devout spirit, often to comfort them. Russians certainly needed comfort in the 1400s. The Tartars and Mongols, invading tribes from Asia, demanded tribute in money and goods. Towns competed for trade, dividing the countryside; with no source of protection, Russians by the thousands were captured as slaves and carried away to southwest Asia.

It took centuries for the Russians to free themselves from the threat of the Mongols and the Tartars. Leaders of the city of Moscow defeated a Mongol army at Kulikovo,

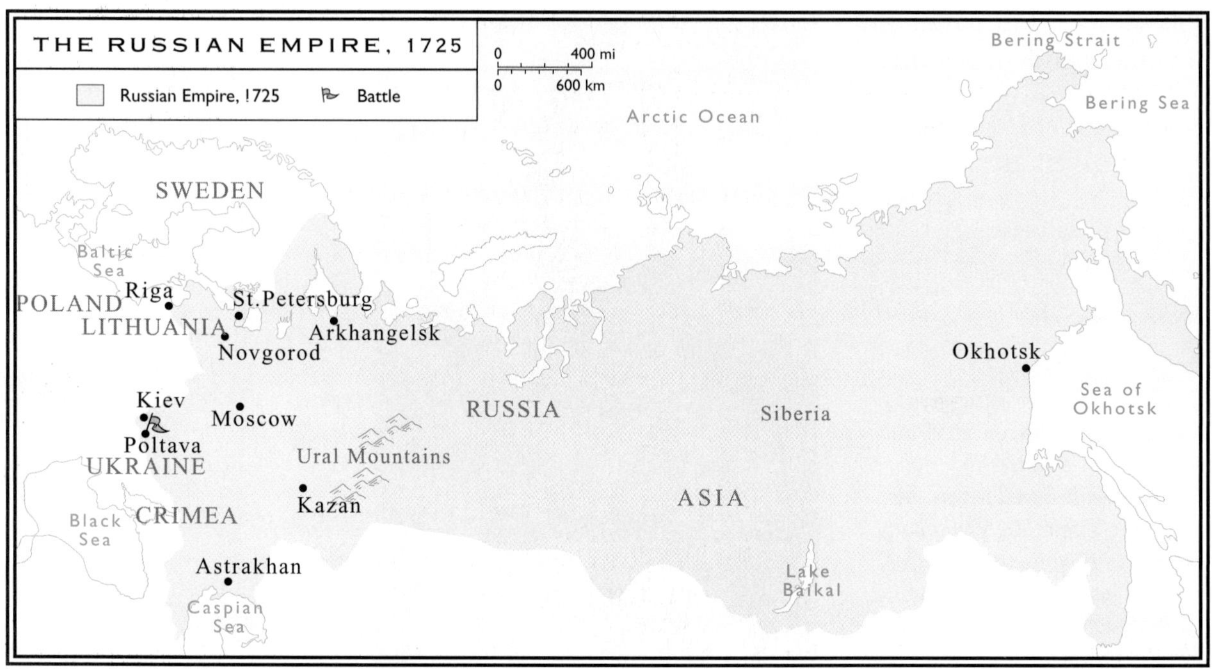

Russia, in 1380, but the Tartars still raided towns and blocked access to the Black Sea. In 1501, a Tartar raid began with an order from their khan demanding that every Tartar man over 15 show up with three horses each, and every five people with a cart. The multiple horses allowed riders to mount quick, long-range attacks, and the carts were to carry the looted goods and captives. So many thousands of Russians and Ukrainians were captured and sold in the Middle East that Russia became second only to West Africa as a source of slaves.

Dimitri Domskoi leads his Russian troops into battle at Kulikovo by the Don River to defeat the Golden Horde in 1380. Dimitri, the grand prince of Moscow, had not yet united Russia, and the Golden Horde still remained a threat, but victory at Kulikovo using Mongol tactics marked the first step toward reaching those goals.

In one Russian expedition to the Crimea in 1687, between 40,000 and 50,000 men were reported lost while trying to establish trading routes on the Black Sea. A Russian saying about the armies going to the plains of the south expressed a grim mindset: "Do not boast leaving for the steppe; boast returning from the steppe."

To withstand threats from the Mongols and the Tartars, the Russians unified under the leadership of the city of Moscow. The Mongols themselves, tired of negotiating with many different towns, had made the princes of Moscow their chief tax collectors. The Moscow princes used this advantage and Mongol backing to force other cities into their alliance. Rulers began to take the title "tsar," a Russian word for the Roman title Caesar, and to dream of a larger role for Russia in the world.

The piercing eyes of Ivan the Terrible suggest his troubled personality, which allowed for the callous murder of people who challenged his power. Ever fearful of his enemies, Ivan once wrote to Queen Elizabeth I of England asking for asylum should he need to escape Russia.

FEAR AND RAGE: THE RULE OF IVAN THE TERRIBLE

One of the most controversial of the tsars was Ivan IV, known as Ivan the Terrible. Terrified is a better description, however, of his early years. His father died when he was three, and his mother, ruling in his name, was murdered when Ivan was eight. The boyars, or Russian nobles, took power and neglected him. An Italian architect in Russia, Peter Triazine, wrote: "The present ruler is a child. The boyars do as they please…and are at each other's throats. There is no order in the land." Ivan remembered his childhood this way: "What suffering did I endure through lack of clothing and through hunger. For in all things my will was not my own." Ivan IV was fortunate, however, in Anastasia, the wife that court officials chose for him. She was a gentle, religious person who cared for him, and her common sense helped him to become a good ruler—for a while.

Ivan managed to push back the Tartars from the Russian cities of Kazan and Astrakhan, freeing thousands of Russian prisoners. The capture of these cities opened up Siberia and, with the Strogonov family of wealthy traders, Russia began its long conquest of the northeast. Ivan also used his government to give relief funds to the people of Moscow after a huge fire, and to support Anatasia's interest in the Orthodox Church. The best-known symbol of this religious interest is St. Basil's Cathedral in Moscow. Earlier Russian churches, like those in the city of Novgorod, often looked like fortresses, with thick walls and high, narrow windows. They

St. Basil's Cathedral, with its colorful onion-shaped domes, was built to celebrate the saint's accurate prediction that Ivan the Terrible's troops would defeat the Tartars at Kazan. Historians dispute the legend that Ivan ordered the eyes of the architects put out so they could never surpass the beauty of this church.

were designed as places where people could gather to resist Mongol attacks. But St. Basil's, with its almost playful sets of onion-shaped domes, was built to celebrate a safer world.

Anastasia died in 1560, and Ivan believed that she, like his mother, had been poisoned. Without her restraining influence, Ivan began to see enemies everywhere. He established the *oprichniki,* a special secret police who dressed in black, carrying the symbols of a broom and a dog's head. They were supposed to sweep away and hound Ivan's enemies. For seven years, the *oprichniki* swept into people's homes, dragged nobles away to their deaths without trial, raped women, and looted houses. Brave priests, such as the Moscow leader Filipp, according to church chronicles, tried to make Ivan stop and confronted him: "How long, will you go on spilling the innocent blood of faithful people.... Tartars and heathens and the whole world can say that all peoples have justice and law, but only in Russia do they not exist." Filipp paid for his bravery with his life.

Without real cause, Ivan decided in 1570 that the people of Novgorod were planning to join with the Lithuanians.

Ivan led an army and the *oprichniki* into the city. They brutally tortured the men of Novgorod, and tied women and children together and pushed them into the river. They drowned so many people that it was several months before the river was cleared of bodies.

Ivan's greatest personal tragedy was murdering his elder son, Ivan. When the son tried to protect his pregnant wife from the father's kicking and beating, Ivan the Terrible hit his son with a steel-tipped rod. His son died a few days later; his daughter-in-law suffered a miscarriage, and both she and the baby died. In his 1572 will, he wrote, "My body grows weak, my soul is sick. . . . All have returned me evil for good, hatred for love." His death in 1584 left few to grieve.

RUSSIA LOOKS WESTWARD

After foreign invasions and famines following Ivan the Terrible's death, the boyars decided that the nobleman Mikhail Romanov should rule. Ivan IV's wife, Anastasia, was part of the Romanov family, and Mikhail seemed to share some of her even-tempered qualities. With Mikhail, the Romanovs began a royal dynasty that lasted until the Russian Revolution in 1917.

The most remarkable of the early Romanovs were the father, daughter, and son combination of Alexis, Sophia, and Peter the Great. Alexis was known as the Pious Tsar, and his relatively mild rule was a relief after Ivan IV. His daughter Sophia was never a ruler in her own right, but

"Without any education, without any foreign help, contrary to the intention of his people, clergy and chief ministers, but merely by the strength of his own genius, observation and example."

—Charles Whitworth, English minister to Russia, admiring Peter the Great, *An Account of Russia,* 1710

Ancient heroes and gods celebrate Peter the Great's founding of the city of St. Petersburg on this elaborate map. By choosing to name the city with the Dutch translation of "Peter's city" instead of the Russian Petrograd, Peter conveyed his admiration for Dutch shipbuilding.

when Alexis died in 1676, she ruled temporarily until her half-brother Peter was old enough to take the throne.

Alexis, Sophia, and Peter all saw the need for a modern army. Alexis began to recruit foreign officers, mainly from Germany and Scotland, to train soldiers in new techniques. By 1624, 445 foreign officers had been recruited into the Russian Army. The local population was suspicious of the foreigners. According to one western European observer, the Austrian ambassador's messenger was told on the streets of Moscow, "Ye, German dogs! . . . the day is at hand when you shall suffer."

Alexis, Sophia, and Peter knew, however, that Russia needed Western knowledge. Russia had no formal schools except for those training the Orthodox clergy. There were no universities, and printers mainly published religious documents. Some foreigners believed that the tsars deliberately kept the Russian people ignorant so they would be easier to control. Giles Fletcher, an English diplomat, observed, "They are kept from traveling, that they may learn nothing, nor see the fashions of other countries abroad." Yet Alexis, Sophia, and Peter were themselves attracted to the West. Alexis began to have plays put on in his court, and his granddaughter Natalya started the first public theater troupe.

A group of religious conservatives known as the Old Believers resisted change the most. Alexis, Sophia, and Peter came down on their resistance harshly. Sophia sent 20,000 of the Old Believers into exile in Siberia. Their leader, Avvakum, had time to write of his experiences before he was tortured and executed. Much of the settlement of Siberia, including the forts and towns built there, was done by the labor he described: "That spring [1657] we began to sail on [lumber] rafts down the Ingoda River.... There was nothing to eat; men died of hunger, and from working in the water. Shallow was the river and the rafts heavy, the taskmasters pitiless,...the cudgels knotty, the whips cutting,...One more stroke and a man would fall dead. Alas, what times were these!"

Old Believers were not the only resisters put down by Alexis, Sophia and Peter. Peasants and the *strelsty*, the old musketeers of the Russian Army, revolted. The *strelsty* raged through the Kremlin, Moscow's fortress complex, and, before the horrified eyes of Sophia and Peter, literally tore apart some of the rulers' relatives. Sophia and others managed, eventually, to get the *strelsty* under control, but Peter planned revenge.

"Old Moscow's paled before this other metropolis: it's just the same as when a widowed Empress Mother bows to a young Tsaritsa's claim."

—Russian poet Aleksandr Pushkin, describing the relationship between Moscow and St. Petersburg, "The Bronze Horseman," 1833

A troika, a sleigh drawn by a team of three horses, was the easiest way for the nobility to travel in the harsh Russian winter. As the empire expanded, Russians tried to avoid traveling in the spring, when thick mud made roads almost impossible to use.

To form a stronger central government able to withstand such revolts, these reforming tsars hired more foreigners to teach accounting, record keeping, and foreign languages. New military equipment could now be ordered from the West more easily than before and used in organized training drills. Peter carried these reforms further by providing a system in which people with ability could reach the top levels of government, and even into the nobility, through hard work and competence. These new officials gradually eroded the power of the boyars.

Besides keeping the peace at home, Alexis and his children wanted to expand Russia. Peter moved his army into Lithuania and attacked Riga in Latvia, but could not take it from the Swedes. His soldiers made up a song about the long siege and casualties there in 1656: "Do not leave us, poor men, to besiege Riga. Riga has already wearied us. Riga has tired us; Riga has plagued us. We have suffered much cold and hunger there."

When Peter took power from his half-sister Sophia in 1696, Russia was on its way toward being a stronger, more forward-looking nation. But Peter, an impatient and imposing man nearly six feet seven inches tall, wanted a faster pace. He planned not just reform, but a new Russia.

Partially disguised in simple clothing as a ship worker so he would not have to go through tedious court ceremonies,

Tall, Dark, and Handsome

SOPHIA, ELECTRESS OF HANOVER, LETTER ABOUT PETER THE GREAT, 1687

This is a description of Peter the Great from a letter written by Sophia, electress of Hanover, in northern Germany, who invited Peter to dinner at her home in 1687. At that time, Peter was on his Great Embassy or trip to western Europe. Sophia Charlotte, the electress's daughter, was known for her wit and beauty, so the evening went probably better than Peter, who disliked formal occasions, expected. As they danced he felt the whalebones in her corsets. "These German women have Devilish hard bones," he shouted, teasing her.

The Tsar is very tall, his features are fine, and his figure very noble. He has a great vivacity of mind, and a ready and just repartee. But, with all the advantages with which nature has endowed him, it could be wished that his manners were a little less rustic [coarse, untrained]. We immediately sat down to table. He was very gay, very talkative, and we established a great friendship for each other, and he exchanged snuff-boxes with my daughter. We stayed in truth a very long time at table, but we would gladly have remained there longer still without feeling a moment of boredom, for the Tsar was in a very good humor and never ceased talking to us. My daughters had her Italians sing. Their song pleased him though he confessed to us that he did not care much for music.

I asked him if he liked hunting. He replied that his father had been very fond of it, but that he himself, from his earliest youth, had a real passion for navigation and fireworks. He told us that he worked himself in building ships, showed us his hands, and made us touch the callous places that had been caused by work. . . .

We regretted that we could not stay much longer. . . . He is a very extraordinary man. . . . He has a very good heart. . . . I must tell you also, that he did not get drunk in our presence, but we had hardly left when the people of his suite began to make ample amends. He is a prince at once very good and very bad. . . . If he had received a better education, he would be an exceptional man, for he has great qualities and unlimited natural intelligence.

Peter went to Europe on a Great Embassy, or trip, to see what ideas and technologies he could bring back. Working with ordinary shipbuilders, he learned modern shipbuilding in Holland. In England, the Royal Navy took him out for war games on the Thames River and let him maneuver one of the ships. John Perry, an Englishman who knew Peter well, wrote: "His Majesty [Peter the Great] has often declared to his lords, when he has been a little merry, that he thinks it a much happier life to be an admiral in England than a tsar in Russia." Peter used these experiences to build the first real Russian navy.

Peter's observations of Western women formed another part of his ideas for change. Upper-class Russian women were generally kept in the *terem,* a secluded part of the home or palace. According to the Domonstroi, a Russian Orthodox religious document of the time, women were supposed to be completely submissive to their husbands. At weddings, the bride's father would give the groom a whip, for the Domonstroi said even a good wife might be whipped.

Peter rebelled against all these customs, perhaps because he found his Russian wife, Evdokia, so dull and old-fashioned. He eventually divorced her and married a

"Are we then born less blest than other nations that the divinity should have infused inept minds into our bodies. Have we not hands? Have we not eyes? . . . By Hercules! We have the same minds, we can do like other folk if we only will it."

—Johann Korb, Austrian diplomatic secretary, quoting Peter the Great about introducing Western-style education to Russians, *Diary of an Austrian Secretary of Legation at the court of the Czar Peter the Great,* 1698

Fountains play before Peter the Great's imposing palace, Peterhof. Peter loved jokes, and visitors strolling the grounds might innocently step on a rock only to trigger a geyser spraying water into the air.

Lithuanian orphan, Catherine. He insisted that officials bring their wives out of the *terem* and that they attend parties and ceremonies in Western-style clothes. New laws made marriage without the bride's consent illegal, and women gained more rights to control their own property.

Peter also put through reforms for men. He wanted them dressed as Westerners—no beards—and educated in secular schools where science and mathematics were emphasized. He sent nobles to Europe—even a 52-year-old, married grandfather—to attend universities.

Above all, Peter wanted a Western city on the Baltic Sea. In order to gain what later became St. Petersburg, he faced two problems. First, the Swedes controlled the land on the Neva River that he had in mind as its site. At the Battle of Poltava in 1709, Peter's army decisively defeated the Swedes in what is now Ukraine. Delighted, Peter wrote a letter to his wife, Catherine, exclaiming: "In a word, the whole of the enemy's army is knocked on the head."

Peter the Great, a tall and imposing figure, oversees the work of several men who seem to be surveying land.

The other problem was that St. Petersburg was a marshy swamp, and not many people wanted to go there. To force Russians to relocate, Peter moved the capital from Moscow to St. Petersburg. Peter forced and bribed workers to drain the marshes into canals. As many as 50,000 workers died building the city. Yet many visitors were impressed by how quickly St. Petersburg grew. A German, Friedrich Weber, wrote in 1714: "When I arrived there, I was expected to find . . . a heap of villages linked together like a plantation in the West Indies . . . however, St. Petersburg may with reason be looked upon as a wonder of the world considering its palaces, sixty-odd thousand houses and the short time that was employed in the building of it."

Just as with the workers' deaths during the building of St. Petersburg, other parts of Peter's reign showed his darker side. When Peter was in Europe, the *strelsty* revolted again, and some supported Sophia's return to power. Peter put down the revolt with torture, public executions, and the imprisonment of Sophia. Like Ivan the Terrible, Peter also killed his son and heir. While Ivan did so in a temper tantrum, Peter had his son Alexis tried for treason, tortured, and hurt so badly that Alexis died. Peter saw Alexis as a lazy, inept person who drank too much and did too little. In 1717, Peter wrote his son a scathing letter that "everything is useless, purposeless" about him. Alexis was like "a gangrenous [diseased] limb. . . . I would rather have an honest stranger than a ne'er-do-well of my own blood" to take the throne. After Alexis ran off to Europe and talked of overturning his father's reforms, Peter decided to bring charges of treason. Alexis died in prison in 1718.

Peter's daughter Elizabeth, almost as energetic and curious as he, continued his Westernization of Russia, though with more tolerance. She tried to outlaw the death penalty in Russia and the torture of people under age 17. Her main interest was in architecture and art. She financed buildings such as the Winter Palace, now a part of the Hermitage, one of the great art museums of the world. The changes to the Summer Palace outside of St. Petersburg in Tsarskoe Selo made it one of the most elaborate palaces of Europe. The building, with its gilded chapel domes peeking over blue walls, was a statement of how far Russia had come from those fortress churches of Novgorod, and how many tears a great empire had wrung from its people to get there.

"Take this book, thou clever boy
And start to climb from the lowest to the topmost steps.
Be not lazy or careless in thy studies
And always pay attention to thy teacher. . .
Begin with the letter A that thou seest here.
Afterward, under teacher's guidance, thou wilt proceed to others."

—Priest Filaret, textbook, 1632

CHAPTER 5

THE REAL MUGHALS, NOT THE REEL MOGULS

EMPIRE IN INDIA

In the early days of Hollywood, movie producers often showed the power of the new media by creating lavish historical films. Elephants, huge buildings, bejeweled actors, and columned throne rooms flashed onto the screen. Because these producers had almost absolute control over the choice of actors, the settings of the films, and the cost, they became known as Hollywood moguls, named after the Mughals of India, who ruled from 1526 until the mid-19th century. The Mughals themselves were named after the Mongols, the central Asian tribe from whom they were partly descended.

The real Mughals, not the movie-reel moguls, had more than just a few elephants to parade by the camera. Akbar, the greatest of the Mughal emperors, who reigned in the

The latticed windows of the Red Fort in Delhi, India, so-called because it was built from red sandstone, are surrounded by ornamental designs and colorful tiles. The Mughals, who built the fort in the 17th century, delighted in displays of art and wealth.

16th and 17th centuries, owned a stable of 5,000 of them. Mughal buildings were not just fronts, like Hollywood sets, but some of the greatest architecture in world history. In India, the Red Fort at Delhi, the Jami Mosque at Agra, and above all, the Taj Mahal, are still visited by millions of people every year. Though actors wore fake jewelry, the Mughal emperors wore the Koh-i-Nur diamond, the largest in the world. Sir Thomas Roe, the English ambassador to Emperor Jahangir's court in the early part of the 17th century, saw him "clothed, or rather laden with diamonds, rubies, pearls. . . . His head, neck, breast, arms, above the elbows, at wrists, his fingers every one, with at least two or three rings . . . rubies as great as walnuts, some greater, such as my eyes were amazed at."

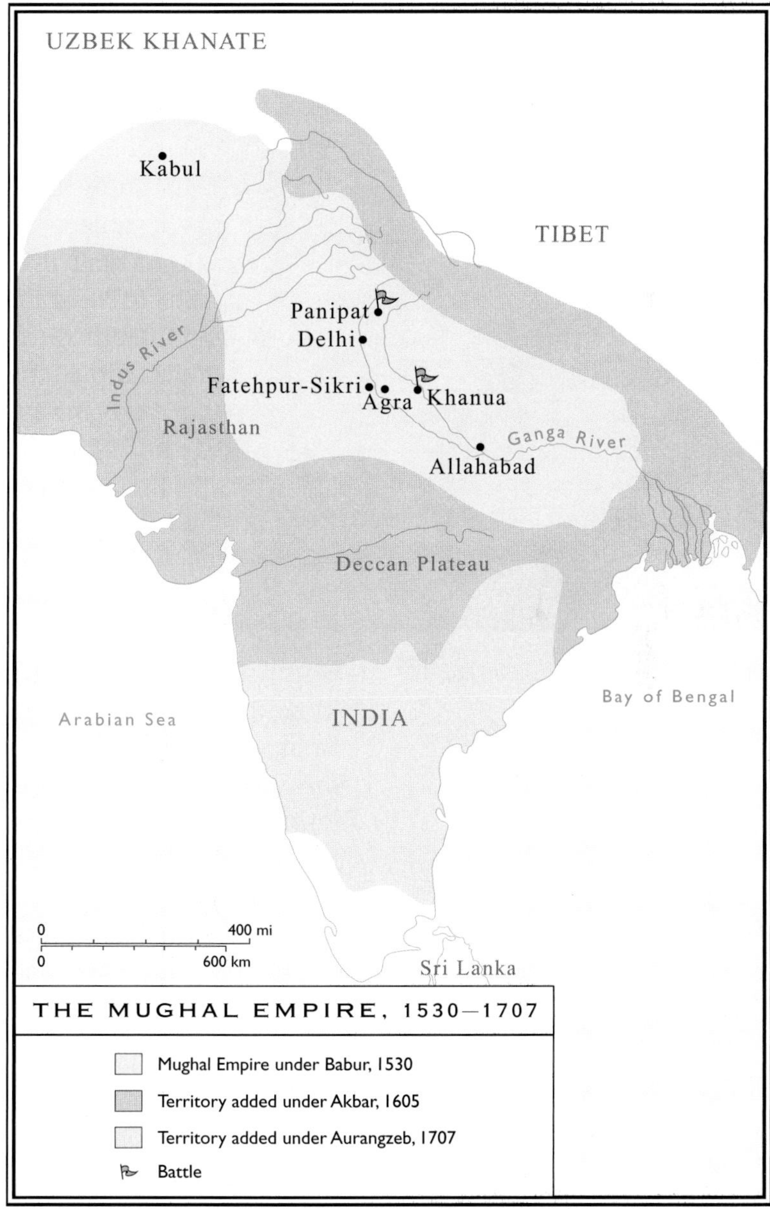

THE MUGHAL EMPIRE, 1530–1707

Yet in some ways, the Mughals were like those Hollywood moguls who lived in a world of make-believe and show. The Mughal display of wealth was meant to awe and encourage submission. Behind the pomp, however, lay injustice and instability. A mere 655 people owned 61 percent of the wealth of the empire. Most of the population lived in backbreaking poverty. The Dutch geographer Joannes de Laet wrote, "The condition of the common people in India is miserable . . . their huts are low, built of generally of mud."

Babur, the founder of the Mughal Empire, consults with his advisers in his palace. Although he generally preferred his gardens to the confines of the royal chambers, Babur was fond of some luxury and complained about campaigns in the southern part of India. In the south, he claimed, there were "no good horses, no good dogs, no grapes, no ice or cold water, no hot baths."

They ate mainly rice and vegetables, sharing a meal from one family bowl, and had almost no clothing or furniture, he noted. According to the French doctor François Bernier in his *Travels in the Mogul Empire*, the burden of taxes made Indian peasants think, "Why should I toil for a tyrant who may come tomorrow and lay his [greedy] hands on all I possess?"

Disruption behind the scenes agitated the Mughal lands. Paintings of the court show the emperor seated calmly, with his subjects looking up to him in rapt attention. The truth was that plots filled the court. Most emperors spent much of their time leading armies and fighting to hold the empire together. Akbar alone put down 144 rebellions during his reign.

BABUR THE TIGER TAKES INDIA

Originally from Central Asia, the Mughals were a Turkish people of the Muslim religion who had raided northern India over the centuries. In 1526, they conquered the Sultanate—or kingdom—of Delhi, their Muslim rivals, and took northern India; soon they also moved into southern India. Though they were Muslims, most of their subjects, including the Rajputs of northern India and the Marathas of southern India, were Hindu and often difficult to control.

A major threat to peace came from within the Mughal dynasty itself. The eldest son did not automatically inherit the throne, and all brothers and sons could compete for the crown. The rivalries were so fierce that they often started early. As de Laet found, "Sons cannot wait for their parents' death but fight amongst themselves and against their parents." Of the six major Mughal rulers, four had their sons rebel against them. Usually the sons lost; 89 were blinded, imprisoned, or killed by their fathers. Shah Jahan, the builder of the Taj Mahal, supported a losing son and was imprisoned by another for the rest of his life.

The first of the Mughal emperors was Zahiruddin Muhammad, nicknamed Babur, "the Tiger." He began his rule in 1494, and true to his nickname, he was a determined warrior. He tried four times to defeat the Sultanate of Delhi and the Rajputs of present-day Rajasthan, in northwest India before he finally succeeded on the fifth try. Also a poet, Babur wrote a couplet about the many defeats, betrayals, and hardships he experienced in his life: "Is there one cruel turn of Fortune's wheel unknown of me? Is there a pang, a grief my wounded heart has missed?"

In his memoirs, Babur wrote about the qualities that enabled him to succeed. When he was caught with his soldiers in a ferocious snowstorm in an Afghan mountain pass, his lieutenants urged him to seek refuge in a cave. "Some of my men in the snow and storm and I in the comfort of a warm home!" Babur recounted with indignation. "The whole horde outside in misery and pain, I inside sleeping at ease! [That] would be far from a man's act, quite another matter than comradeship. Whatever hardship... there is, I will face; where strong men stand, I will stand."

Babur's men also knew that, when victorious, they would get most of the plunder. After the victories at Panipat (1526) and Khanus (1527) in northern India, when "the treasures of five kings fell into his hands," his daughter Gulbadan Begum wrote, "he gave everything away." Loyal troops were loyally rewarded.

A network of women looked after Babur and helped to advance his career. Officially kept out of politics, elite Muslim women exercised considerable power through family connections. In his autobiography, Babur praised his grandmother Asian-daulat Begun: "She was very wise and far sighted and most affairs of mine were carried under her advice." His mother traveled with him throughout his early trials, and a group of aunts sheltered him when, defeated, he had no place else to go.

Babur also learned from his enemies and from his mistakes. Unlike his Hindu rivals, the Rajputs, he used new

"Your peasants are down-trodden; the yield of every village has declined. It is a reign in which the army is in ferment, the merchants complain; the Muslims cry, the Hindus are grilled; most men lack bread at night and in the daytime inflame their own cheeks by slapping them [in anguish]."

—Shivaji, leader of the Hindu Maratha resistance against the Mughals

Babur, on horseback, leads his forces against other Central Asian tribes in the mountains. Though he left the battlefield as often in defeat as in victory, he was a determined fighter, explaining, "Give me but fame and if I die I am contented. If fame be mine, let Death claim my body."

artillery strategies to fit the new, more powerful cannons. The Uzbeks from Central Asia had developed massed firing of artillery, and Babur imitated their strategy in the Battle of Panipat in 1526. He also tried to better himself as a leader. His own writings are fairly frank about his life, and he admits to drinking wine, forbidden to Muslims, to excess. Before the Battle of Panipat, he told his troops that, to gain victory, he had made a solemn vow never to drink wine again. His troops responded with cheers, knowing that he was now really serious.

Babur's son, Humayun, almost lost everything when he was defeated by the Afghans. Then, in 1554, with Persian help, the most gifted Mughal emperor of all, Babur's grandson Akbar, claimed the throne. One British officer, Sir William Sleeman, claimed, "Akbar has always appeared to me among sovereigns what Shakespeare was among poets."

Through war and diplomacy, Akbar expanded the Mughal Empire into new Indian territories. Besides being a good military leader, he had a vision of empire that included all his subjects. As the Jesuit priest Jerome Xavier wrote: "He was great with the great and lowly with the lowly." Akbar promoted religious tolerance between Muslims, Hindus, Sikhs, and Christians. He repealed the *jizya* (a special tax on non-Muslims), married a Rajput Hindu princess, and allowed the building of new Hindu and Sikh temples. Toward the end of his life, he even tried to combine religions into a new one he called Din-i-Ilahi, or Divine Faith. To promote justice, he reformed land taxes so that they were based on what the land could produce, especially in drought years.

Despite all his talents, there was one thing Akbar could not do: read. He had to have all documents read to him. His

Finding a Birthday Bargain

FRANÇOIS BERNIER, TRAVELS IN THE MOGUL EMPIRE, 1670

Twice a year, for the emperor's birthday and Nauroz (a spring festival), the Mughal emperors held fairs for women of the royal harem. François Bernier, a French doctor to the Mughal court, described in his 1670 book, Travels in the Mogul Empire, *this "whimsical kind of fair." Here various levels of society mixed, young women were displayed as potential marriage partners, and the tensions of the court were forgotten. Bernier offers a lighter version of an emperor's life and also takes up the theme of Muslim women's interest in economics and ability to control their own property.*

It [the fair] is conducted by the handsomest and most engaging wives of the [officials]. The articles exhibited are beautiful brocades, rich embroideries of the newest fashion, turbans elegantly worked on cloth of gold, fine muslins... and other articles of high price. These bewitching females act the part of traders, while the purchasers are the King, the Begums or Princesses and other distinguished ladies of the Seraglio [harem]. If any Omrah's [official's] wife happens to have a handsome daughter, she never fails to accompany her mother that she may be seen by the King and become known to the Begums.

The charm of this fair is the most ludicrous manner in which the King makes his bargains, frequently disputing the value of a penny. He pretends that the good lady cannot possibly be in earnest... and that positively he will give no more than such a price. The woman, on the other hand, endeavors to see to the best advantage and when the King perseveres in offering what she considers too little money, high words frequently ensue and she fearlessly tells him that he is a worthless trader... The Begums betray, if possible, a still greater anxiety to be served cheaply; high words are heard on every side, and the loud and scurrilous quarrels of the seller and buyers create a complete farce. But sooner or later they agree upon the price, the Princesses, as well as the King, buy right and left, pay in ready money and often slip out of their hands, as if by accident, a few gold instead of silver rupees, intended as a compliment to the fair merchant or her pretty daughter. The present is received in the same unconscious manner, and the whole ends amidst witty jest and good-humor.

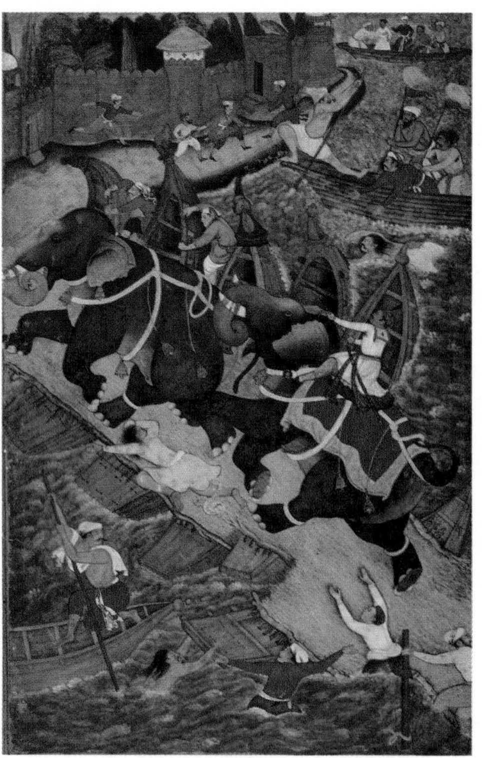

Mughal emperor Akbar rides after a runaway elephant as onlookers scramble to avoid the chase. As part of their new war tactics, the Mughals began to use elephants instead of horses in shock attacks. Most mounted soldiers, however, still kept horses handy to jump onto for quick pursuit of their enemies.

early life provided little space for quiet learning. Akbar had been left behind with relatives and shifted from place to place. The lowest point of Akbar's life was when he was five, and an uncle held him captive. When Akbar's father attacked the rebellious uncle's fort, Akbar's uncle dangled him over the ramparts so his father would not fire on the fort's walls.

Akbar remained tolerant and fairly easygoing, even toward animals, in spite of his early hardships. In an era when most Muslims avoided dogs as unclean, Akbar enjoyed them and had kennels filled with different breeds, an upsetting sight to the strict Muslim leaders. Marrying a Hindu wife, allowing Sikh temples, petting dogs—some Muslims began to worry about Akbar's beliefs. However, Akbar's curiosity, whether about religion, animals, painting, poetry, or war, impressed foreign observers. The Jesuit priest Anthony Monserrate wrote of him: "The eyes are small but extremely vivid and when he looks at you it seems as if they hurt you with their brightness."

AN EMPIRE WITHERS

The Mughal emperors who followed lacked the exceptional natures of Babur and Akbar. Akbar's son, Jahangir, devoted himself to art and wine, and turned over most government decisions to his able wife, Nur Jahan. Jahangir's son, Shah Jahan, ruled fairly well, but his private life turned into a family nightmare that began the decline of the Mughals. Though he had several wives, he deeply loved one, Mumtaz Mahal. After Mumtaz's death during childbirth, Shah Jahan

> *"We associate at convenient seasons with learned men of all religions and thus derive profit from their exquisite discourses and exalted aspirations."*
>
> —Akbar, letter to Philip II of Spain, describing religious tolerance in Akbar's empire, 1582

was devastated. He built a tomb for her, the exquisite building known as the Taj Mahal.

The calm serenity of the Taj Mahal was, however, quite different than the family Mumtaz Mahal left behind. Without Mumtaz Mahal's calming presence, the family split into competing factions. Following intrigue and ruthless fighting, Jahan's most relentless son, Aurangzeb, won. Aurangzeb executed his brother and imprisoned his father, Shah Jahan, and sister, Jahanara. The father wrote to his son, "Only yesterday I was master of nine hundred thousand troopers, but today I

Shah Jahan built the Taj Mahal as a memorial to his beloved wife Mumtaz Mahal, who died while giving birth to her 14th child. The Taj, with its white marble, reflecting pools, and gardens, was designed to convey the Islamic view of a beautiful afterlife.

A 16th-century gold spoon, inset with rubies, emeralds, and diamonds, combines utility and elegance. To better appreciate skilled arts, each Mughal emperor trained in a particular craft; Akbar, for example, was both a warrior and a lace maker.

am in need of a pitcher of water!" In a curt written reply, Aurangzeb answered, "It is your own doing."

Aurangzeb, the last of the major Mughal rulers, had the fighting ability of his ancestors, but a sour disposition, and he lacked the tolerance of his grandfather Akbar. He brought back the tax on non-Muslims, tore down some major Hindu temples, and outlawed music and dancing. He plunged into a disastrous war to conquer the Deccan plateau, the southern part of India. This warfare drained the land of wealth and people. An Italian traveler, Niccolao Manucci, reported that "the War never ceases. . . . The country is so desolate and depopulated that neither fire nor light can be found in the course of three or four days' journey." Just as he had done to his father, Aurangzeb's sons and a daughter rebelled against him. At the end of his life, Aurangzeb wrote to his officials, "I am forlorn and destitute and misery is my ultimate lot." In another letter to them, he lamented, "My life has been wasted in vain!"

Aurangzeb's gloomy view of his reign does not represent the general view of the Mughal Empire. The Mughals left lasting achievements. At its height, their empire encouraged trade, opened roads, built cities, and established standard weights and measures and trustworthy coins. Under the Mughals, Indian textiles such as calico and madras cotton became known throughout the world, and international trade brought silver and gold into the empire.

The Mughals also left behind splendid architecture and art that borrows from Persian, Central Asian, and Hindu

"A monarch should be ever intent on conquest, otherwise his enemies rise in arms against him. The army should be exercised in warfare, lest from want of training they become self-indulgent."

—Akbar, *Fifth Book of the Akbar-nama,* late 16th century

sources. Although the Taj Mahal is the best known of the Mughal buildings, Akbar's Red Fort at Agra combines military defense, style, and vivid color.

Mughal painters mainly worked on portraits or illustrated manuscripts. According to strict Muslim beliefs, artists are not to represent living things, whether animals or people. In contrast, the Mughals followed a Persian tradition that some human representation in painting was permissible. The opening line in one of Babur's poems: "Let your portrait flatter you never so much than it you more," indicated that the portrait should be realistic, not idealized.

Mughal women dine and converse in court. Although they were segregated to their own part of the palace, women were often highly educated and wrote poetry, histories, and religious commentary.

"Prosperity and bad luck depend on four things; first, upon your wife; second upon your slave; third upon your house; four upon your horse."

—Jahangir, Emperor and husband to Nur Jahan, who ran much of his administration, *Jahangirnama,* 17th century

Mughal artists were not shy about showing women in their art. The painter Abu-Hasan, for example, showed Jahangir's wife Nur Jahan with a rifle in her hands to commemorate her shooting of four tigers in six shots.

Though strict Muslim tradition placed women in a harem, hidden in a separate part of the house, Mughal women often had powerful careers. Akbar's wife Salima Sultan Begum managed to reconcile her son with the emperor to prevent civil war. Jahanara, daughter of Shah Jahan, at different points in her life, pleaded for the lives of her four brothers and father. The emperor Jahangir went so far as to have his wife Nur Jahan issue edicts on her own, and minted coins with her image. She would later lead troops into battle, shooting arrows while mounted on an elephant.

One of the reasons why Mughal women could be involved more in political life is that they were generally well educated, sometimes more than their battle-trained brothers. Jahanara wrote poetry and a history of Muslim mystic saints. Aurangzeb's daughter, Zeb-un-Nissa, was so well trained in the Quran that she wanted to write a commentary on it, but her intolerant father made her stop.

Unlike most European women at that time, Muslim women could control their own property, even when they married, and they could also inherit from their fathers' estates. Some of the royal women became quite wealthy. Nur Jahan, who invested in international trade, made deals with the Portuguese and English.

The Mughals saw themselves as bringing a more enlightened spirit to India, which is reflected in their appreciation of books and writing. After receiving a letter from his son Humayun, Babur wrote back, "In the future, write without elaboration; use plain, clear words so your trouble and your readers' will be less." Akbar collected a library of 24,000 books, even though he could only have them read to him. For Akbar, these books represented not only the past but also the future. Other nations' books were important, he said: "Truly, we must not reject a thing that has been adopted by the wise men of other nations merely because we cannot find it in our book, or how shall we progress?"

The Mughal Empire left us with lasting images in art and architecture of what wealth and power—mogul or Mughal—could be, but by the early 1700s they had lost center stage. They had not used their wealth to advance their country's agricultural or educational systems, scientific research, or naval power. They founded no major universities, nor sent envoys abroad to see European technology in action. After three centuries of rule, they faded as European powers, especially the British, stepped into India.

Illustrations of antelopes appear in Akbar's personal copy of his grandfather's autobiography. Although Akbar himself could not read, he appreciated Babur's realistic descriptions of the world and his belief that "every act should be recorded precisely as it occurred."

CHAPTER 6

TRIUMPH OF THE TURKS

THE RISE OF THE OTTOMAN EMPIRE

The Ottoman Empire was full of contradictions. For one thing, the Ottoman's homeland was not in Turkey but on the steppes of Central Asia. After migrating west in tribal groups to fight the Mongols, they established themselves in Anatolia, the central region of Asia Minor. There, as Muslims, they confronted the Byzantines, the major power in that part of the world. Living in the eastern part of the old Roman Empire with their capital at Constantinople, the Byzantines, who were Greek Orthodox and Armenian Christians, considered themselves the last Romans. After defeating the Byzantines at Manzikert (now in Turkey) in 1071, the Turks began a long campaign to take all of the peninsula of Asia Minor, and eventually much of the Balkans and the Middle East. Their empire, which was finally unified around 1300, would last more than 600 years, until 1923.

A Portuguese map of Constantinople reveals where the defenders most expected attacks: double walls to the west and higher walls facing the land bridge in the north contrast with shorter fortifications to the south and east.

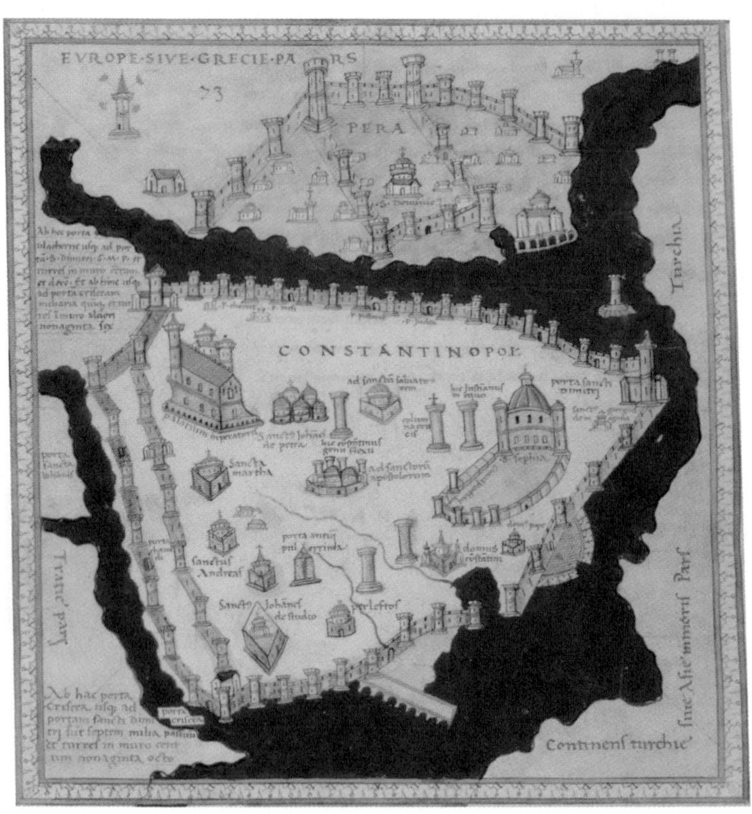

Even though Muslim Turkish warriors manned the Ottoman Army, former Christians from southern Europe, not Turks, comprised the most elite corps of the army and many occupied top government posts. Turkish leaders, called sultans, expanded the Ottoman Empire to spread the Islamic religion, yet at the same time practiced tolerance in religion and allowed Christians and

Jews places in their society. Even though the sultans, like the Mughals, kept the women of their families secluded in a harem, the valide sultan, the sultan's mother, was at times leader of the empire.

RULE BY THE SWORD

Orhan, the first major Turkish sultan, became so powerful that he was able to demand and receive the hand of one of the Byzantine princesses, Nilufer Hatun, in marriage. She converted to Islam. A talented woman, she even ruled the Ottoman Empire when Orhan was on campaign with his army.

Beyazit I, known as the Thunderbolt because of the speed with which he could move his army, was one of the most intriguing sultans to follow Orhan. An impetuous warrior, he fought in three of the most important battles in Ottoman history. The first of these was in 1387 at Kosovo, a name that still echoes in Serbian history as the sad "place of the blackbirds" (the blackbirds that feasted on the Serbian dead).

Before the battle, rival factions within the Serbian army had a dispute about one man's bravery. To prove he was not a coward, the Serb went to the Turkish camp and claimed to be a traitor. When he was taken to the sultan's tent for questioning, he stabbed Murad, Beyazit's father. As his father lay dying, Beyazit threw himself into fighting, and his outnumbered Ottoman forces defeated the Serbs. They captured the Serbian king Lazar and brought him before the dying Murad, who ordered his execution. Serbia was put under Ottoman control, and in a twist of fate,

A steel saber, covered with gold flowers and once inlaid with rubies, may have been made for the sultan Suleyman the Magnificent. Verses of the Quran chiseled into the blade refer to the magical powers of King Solomon and victory in a holy war.

"For fear of God I mustn't tell lies,
for fear of the beg [Turkish governor]
I mustn't tell the truth.
It's hard to become a kadi [Turkish judge]
but once you've made it, butter and
honey will come on their own. Woe to Bosnia as long as there's a kadi there."

—Bosnian saying, suspecting Turkish officials of corruption, 18th century

The Ottoman sultan and generals in this painting are shown larger than the rest of commanders in camp during the conquest of Georgia, a kingdom in the Caucasus. Georgia was one of the first Christian kingdoms and, under a tolerant Ottoman religious policy, its citizens were allowed to continue worshipping in their own churches.

Stefan Lazarevic and Beyazit, the two sons of the dead leaders, became allies, and Beyazit married Stefan's sister. Many Serbs now found themselves fighting for the Muslim Ottomans, but clearly they did not relish their new role. As one said, "I pray God to help the Christians and that I will be among the first dead in this war."

The second of Beyazit's crucial military tests occurred in modern Bulgaria on the banks of the Danube River at the Battle of Nicopolis in 1396. Here he defeated an alliance of Hungarians, Teutonic Knights, and other European armies. Because Europeans had killed Turkish prisoners before the battle, Beyazit ordered 10,000 European prisoners executed. His troops grumbled that the prisoners would have brought a big profit on the slave markets, but for Beyazit revenge was more important. The Battle of Nicopolis indicated that the Turks intended to stay and expand their power in Europe.

These two victories increased Beyazit's sense of self-importance, but his next opponent, Timur the Lame, knew all the Central Asian tricks of battle. Beyazit had been increasing his power in Anatolia by waging war against local Turkish chiefs, who then appealed to Timur. In a series of angry letters, each man insulted the other. Timur wanted to know why Beyazit was fighting Muslim Turks instead of attacking Christian Byzantium. In response, Beyazit slighted Timur by questioning his royal pedigree. Because Timur, who was from a fairly humble background, had made his historians fake his descent from Genghis Khan, this taunt was deadly. Timur retaliated by sending Beyazit a woman's dress, implying he was too weak to fight.

The two men resolved their differences by the sword in the Battle of Ankara in 1402. Abandoning his usual good battle sense, Beyazit let Timur goad him into attack. His allies included Stefan Lazarevic's Serbs, who fought very well, and the Tartars, who deserted him at a crucial point in the battle. Timur not only beat Beyazit, but captured him, his wife, one son, and Stefan. Timur killed the son, but, not known for his compassion, let the others live—to endure humiliation. His soldiers slashed Beyazit's wife's clothes immodestly and carried Beyazit around on a litter so everyone could insult him. Though Stefan and his sister (Beyazit's wife) were later released, Timur kept Beyazit in prison and planned torture for him. Beyazit, not wanting to give Timur that pleasure, killed himself by hitting his head against the prison walls.

Following the defeat at Ankara, Beyazit's sons fought each other for the throne. Mehmet I, the victor, began his reign by constructing grand new mosques so that he could claim God willed his rule. In this, Mehmet copied his father, who built the Yildirum (Thunderbolt) Beyazit Complex in the Turkish city of Bursa, which, with its uniquely shaped Bursa arch, is considered the first real Ottoman-style building. An Ottoman saying was "a Sultan never dies so long as he is building." Memories of battles might fade, but mosques would remind people of past victories and sultans.

"You catch and shackle
the old and the arch-
priests
In order to the take the
children as Janissaries.
Their parents weep and
their sisters and brothers
too
And I cry until it pains me;
As long as I live I shall cry,
For last year it was my son
and this year my brother."

—Christian song, late 15th century

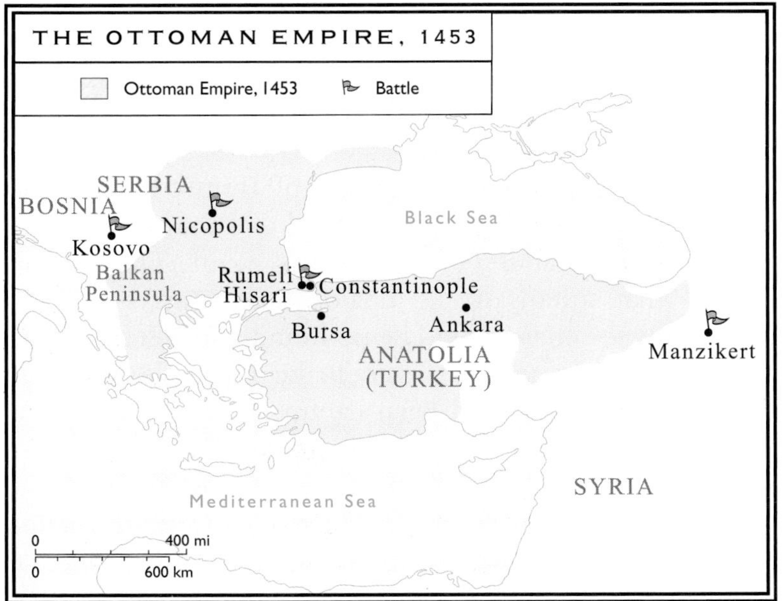

This stern portrait of Mehmet the Conqueror fits the Venetian Giacomo deLanguschi's opinion of him as a person "sparing of laughter and burning with the desire to rule." After angrily watching from shore as his admiral bungled a naval operation, Mehmet once drove his horse into the sea, yelling curses in a fit of rage.

Mehmet I set a bloodthirsty precedent by killing his brothers after he defeated them. His son did the same, and his grandson Mehmet II had the following included in his Code of Laws of the House of Osman: "It is proper that his [the sultan's] brothers, for the sake of the order of the world, be slain." Because the Ottomans had no tradition of the eldest son inheriting the throne, the son who got to the capital first and killed his brothers would now become sultan. As the sultans had children with many concubines, a man who wanted the throne might have to kill several stepbrothers; one sultan killed 19. This chaos resulted in terrible slaughter. Male babies born to the sultan's sisters were killed at birth. About eighty Ottoman princes were killed according to this fratricide, or brother-killing, law. This custom did leave the sultan unchallenged by his relatives, but it also led to intrigues, as none of women of the sultan wanted their sons killed.

According to legend, as a result of Timur's humiliation of Beyazit's wife, later sultans decided that they must never face the public abuse of their wives again. The custom became that sultans would not officially marry—if there were no wives, there would be no humiliation. Instead, the sultan's partners could be said to be merely expendable slaves, women who had been captured and sold at slave markets. Since Muslims were not supposed to make slaves of other Muslims, these women were Christians or Jews, who later converted to Islam. Thus slave women became some of the most powerful people in the empire, especially during the "reign of women," from 1566 to 1666.

When the sultan proved incompetent or absent, the sultan's mother, or valide sultan, might take over power. One of the most powerful of these valide sultans, Kosen, had officials appeal to her: "Gracious mistress, the folly and madness of the Sultan [Ibrahim] have put the world in danger, the infidels have taken forty castles on the frontier of Bosnia . . . while the Sultan thinks only of pleasure." Kosen agreed to have the sultan deposed and tried to shape up the administration, telling one official, "Have I made you vizier [administrative officer] to spend your time in gardens and vineyards? Devote yourself to the affairs of the empire and let me hear of your deportments."

Christian male slaves also became part of the Ottoman court. The Tartar's switch to Timur's side at the Battle of Ankara suggested to the Ottomans that they needed to create a new, more trustworthy army, the Janissaries. To create this force, the Turks imposed a "boy-tax," called the *devsirme* (gathering), every seven years on the Christians in the Balkan part of the Ottoman Empire. The rounding up of these children was often heartbreaking to watch. One European traveler, Bartholomanus Georgiewitz, wrote: "I can find no right words to picture the pain and sorrow, the weeping and wailing of these parents when their children were torn from their bosoms and out of the grasp by those fiends." The boys were converted to Islam and often used to fight against Christians.

The Ottomans, however, saw the *devshirme* differently. The boys were being recruited into two elite organizations where, if they proved themselves, they had great opportunities. The most able were put into schools to learn Turkish, Arabic, and Persian—the three major languages of the lands the Turks ruled—so that they could administer the Ottoman Empire. Forty-three of the first forty-eight grand viziers, the top administrative officers, came from the *devshirme* boys. Despite their power, they were still slaves to the sultan, and he could take their lives or their wealth at any time.

This felt hat, called a ketsche, was the headdress of a Turkish military official. Similar to those worn by Janissaries, it is decorated with a gilded silver tube that would have held a colorful plume.

A second group of boys trained as Janissaries. Europeans were impressed with Janissary discipline; their reputation was that they "came together for war as though they had been invited to a wedding." The sultans intended the Janissaries to be the one absolutely loyal force they could rely on. There were dangers in creating such an elite force, however. When the Janissaries got angry, they would rush out of their barracks, turn over their big community soup kettles, and use them as drums to warn the sultan they were near revolt. Wise sultans listened to their complaints; unwise ones sometimes wound up dead.

Although his court officials, new army, and court women were all enslaved, the sultan had to curry the favor of two main Turkish groups. One was the Turkish landowners, who furnished cavalry troops and horses for military campaigns. The other group was the Ulema, the leaders of the Islamic court system. The Ulema could step in and remind the sultan of his duties and, at times, try to check his excesses. When Ahmet I wanted to build a mosque in his own name, for example, the Ulema told him that he should not take general treasury funds. In this case, Ahmet I overruled the Ulema and built Ahmediye, the Blue Mosque in Istanbul.

Although the official religion of the Ottomans was Islam, they did not try to force this religion on all subjects of the empire, as Christian monarchs of Europe often did at the time. Jews and Christians were considered *dhimmis*, or people of the Book, who shared some of the same biblical history as Muslims. However, by failing to accept Muhammad

"The Turkish armies are like powerful rivers swelled by rain which cause infinite destruction when they find ways of undermining the dikes which hold them back and rush into the breach."

—Habsburg ambassador Ghiselin de Busbecq, letter to his friend Nicholas Michault, 1555–62

An Ottoman officer in a tall hat stands in the center of a public square, deciding which young Christian boys he will choose to join his Janissary corps of elite troops and officials. The selection, called a devshirme, *was heartbreaking for families, but often meant increased opportunity for the boys who were chosen.*

as the Prophet, Christians and Jews had erred in Muslim eyes. Therefore, they could be specially taxed, and they could not try to convert Muslims. Still, they could have their own religious leaders and worship as they liked within their own communities. In 1602, Mehmet III issued a regulation stating the Ottoman position that the "protection and preservation and safeguarding" of the lives of Jews and Christians was a "perpetual and collective duty" of the Muslim community and the sultans.

Tolerance for Christians within the empire, however, did not mean wars against Christians stopped elsewhere. The dream of Turkish sultans had long been to take the city of Constantinople, in Turkey, and finally defeat the Byzantine Empire. What the sultan desired most was Constantinople's strategic position between the Black Sea and the eastern Mediterranean. By 1450, the young, ambitious sultan Mehmet II believed he could seize Constantinople.

THE SACK OF CONSTANTINOPLE

By 1450, the Byzantines were an exhausted empire. The people of Constantinople could raise only 5,000 troops against Mehmet II's 100,000. *The Codex Barberimus Gaecus III,* a Greek chronicle of the 17th century, described the people of Constantinople as follows: "[They]... kept begging God, with tears and sighed; they held religious processions...; barefoot and [with] great reverence did they parade the holy icons. Many people, men, women, children,... confessed their sins and begged the Lord from their souls and hearts, as no other power outside of God could fight against the might of the Turk. So they awaited the day of the assault."

Built in 1452, the fortress of Rumeli Hisari looms over the narrowest point of the Bosphorus, the water entryway to the city of Constantinople. Completed in only four months, the construction of the fort was ordered by Mehmet II to prevent European fleets from sailing up the Bosphorus to aid the city he was determined to conquer.

In spite of its weakened condition, Constantinople was still formidably defended. Its walls were high, thick, and tough to breach. Byzantine women and children throwing rocks down on the Turks joined soldiers to beat back assaults on the wall. Byzantine defenders set ablaze the huge wooden towers the Turks pushed against the walls. Slowly, though, the battle turned in the Turks' favor. A Christian cannon maker named Urban constructed several huge guns for Mehmet; one alone took 60 oxen to pull into place. Firing cannons at one place in the walls weakened them. Mehmet then had some luck when a Byzantine gate was mistakenly left open, and his Janissaries battled their way inside.

The leader of Byzantium, Constantine XI, had known the battle was a losing cause. His final speech to his people reminded them that "you have always fought against the enemies of the Christians bravely.... Know it well, this day will bring you honor.... Prepare yourself for tomorrow; it will be a day of war." Though he might have escaped, Constantine stayed with

The Sultana's Last Wishes

EVLIYA CELEBI, BOOK OF TRAVELS, 17TH CENTURY

Evliya Celebi, who traveled throughout the Ottoman Empire over a 40-year period, was a minor attendant attached to the household of Melek Pasha, one of the sultan Murad IV's major officials. Melek Pasha was married to Murad's daughter, Kaya Sultan, who died at 27. In a biography of Melek, Celebi later wrote of the time he spent with Melek Pasha and Kaya Sultan from 1588 to 1662. When Kaya Sultan was pregnant, she had a dream that foreshadowed her death and she made her will. As a sultana, the daughter of the sultan, and as a Muslim woman who had the property rights to determine the distribution of her own goods, Kaya Sultan's decisions affected many people. Her will illustrates how important the financial arrangements of women from the upper classes were to the mosques and charities of the empire. Kaya Sultan died in childbirth.

The pasha tried to console her in every way possible, but it was no use. The sultana grew more pious day by day. She gave 20,000 gold pieces in trust for Mecca and Medina, and another 20,000 for the benefit of everyone in her household, great and small, including those off campaigning, the cooks, the [painters] and butlers, the falconers and her private staff. She provided in her will that 40,000 prayers be offered up for her soul nightly, stipulating 20,000 gold pieces to her trustee [for this purpose]. She also made provision for her own household retainers. . . . She gave over the deeds of her seventy gardens and vineyards, her summer palaces and estates—in short all of her real property—to her children and to her and Melek's servants, with provision in her will that if the lineage came to an end, all revenue from her properties should go to the Holy Cities. For among the Sultanas of that period, none was wealthier than she. . . .

It is a fact that, of the seventeen sultanas [daughters of the sultan] who were alive in those days, none got on with her husband so well as Kaya with Melek. She was, too, very clever and prudent in managing her household. She was a true daughter of Sultan Murad IV, a raging lioness, and a benefactress to all the other sultanas.

The sixth-century Christian church of Hagia Sophia, or Holy Wisdom, with its massive dome, was a major architectural feat of the Byzantine culture. After Mehmet II conquered Constantinople, he prevented his Ottoman troops from tearing up the cathedral's floors and damaging its pillars, and he ordered that it be converted into a mosque, Aya Sofya.

"Three days after the fall of the city he [Mehmet II] released the ships so that each might sail off to its own province and city, each carrying such a load that it seemed each would sink. And what sort of a cargo: luxurious cloths and textiles, objects and vessels of gold, silver, bronze and brass, books beyond all counting and number, prisoners including priests and lay persons, nuns and monks."

—Greek historian Ducas, describing Turkish ships leaving Constantinople, 15th century

his people. When the end of the fighting was near, he took off his golden helmet and armor and fought to the death anonymously so no enemy could recognize him and mutilate the body of the last emperor of Byzantium. Constantinople surrendered to Mehmet on May 29, 1453. Three days of looting and pillaging followed. Thousands of the city's citizens were sold into slavery throughout the Muslim world.

Mehmet, though proud of his new title, the Conqueror, seemed unsettled by his own victory. He went to the Hagia Sophia, the largest church in Constantinople (today a museum) and before entering, knelt to put earth on his head to show his humility.

A ruined city was not what Mehmet had fought for. He began rebuilding Constantinople with new mosques; a new palace, Topkapisaray; and a new population to balance the Greek Orthodox groups already there. Turks were recruited to come to the city and, according to Ottoman documents, promised "houses and orchards and gardens." When these announcements did not work, Mehmet forced families to come. For Mehmet and many in the Islamic world, the fall of Constantinople was a major triumph. For a Greek monk writing in the monastery of Agorothas, "Nothing worse than this has happened nor will it happen."

CHAPTER 7

WHEN TENTS BECOME TOWERS

THE SULTANS SETTLE DOWN

In 1453, the Ottomans captured Constantinople after a bloody battle. Now that the Turks controlled the Black Sea trade through the Dardanelles, a narrow strait in northwestern Anatolia, they expanded naval control over the Mediterranean and stocked a major supply base for more conquest of Europe. With luck, having captured the second ancient Roman capital, Byzantium, they could strike out for the city of Rome itself. Turkish ships began to raid Venice and other parts of Italy. People started calling the city Istanbul ("to the city") rather than have it bear the name of the Roman emperor, Constantine, who had converted the empire to Christianity. The Turks also realized that a skyline dominated by Christian churches would need changing.

An Ottoman fleet blockades the port of Marseille in southern France, preventing the ships in the harbor from leaving. Under the leadership of the Ottoman admiral Barbarossa, the Turks took over the cities of Marseille, Toulon, and Nice until Francis I of France bribed them to leave.

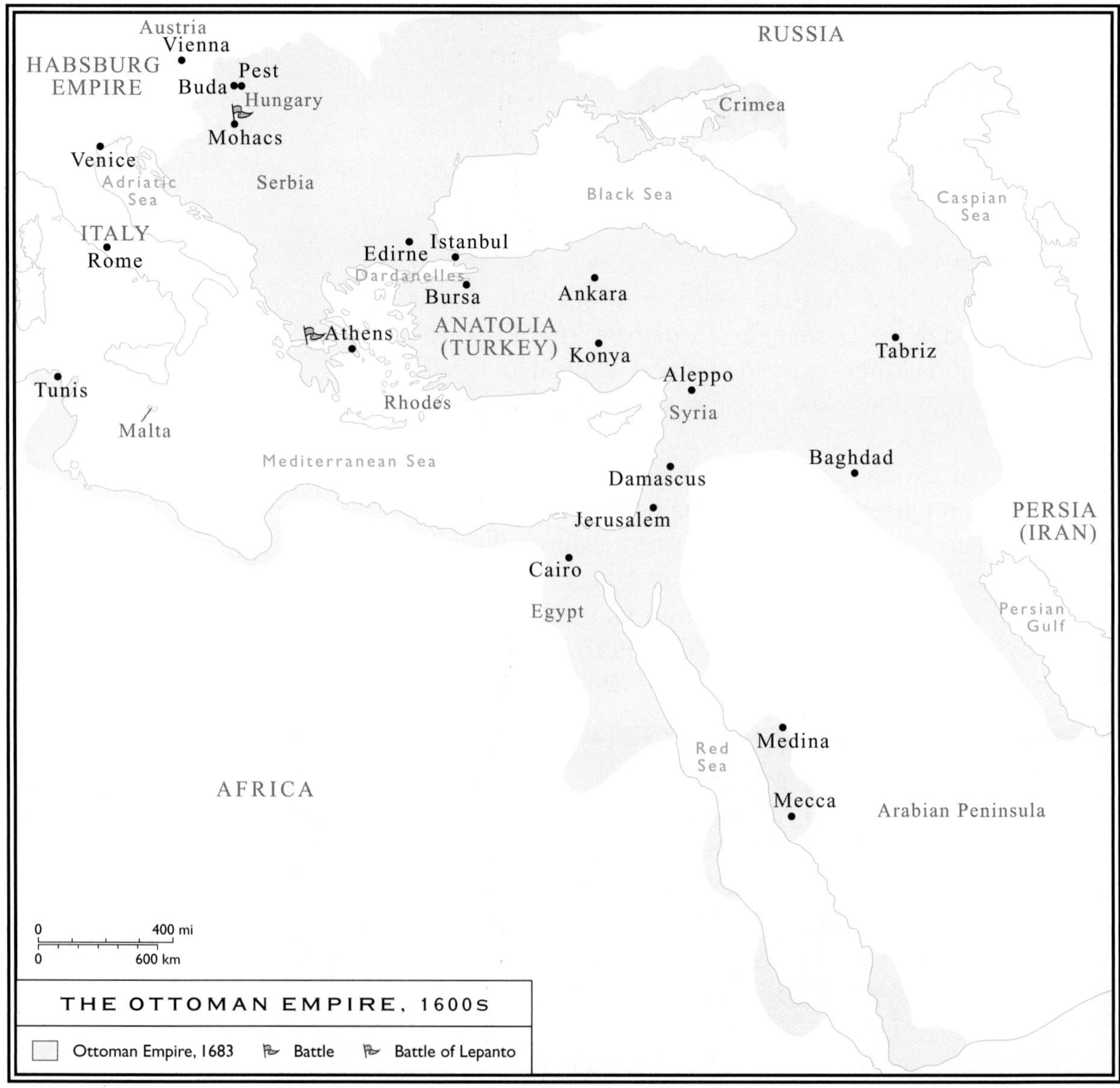

Yet in some ways, Constantinople captured the Turks as well. Traditionally, the Turkish capital was wherever the sultan put up his tent, whether in Konya, Bursa, or Edirne. But Constantinople—Istanbul now—was a tempting place to linger. An early European ambassador, Ogier Ghiselin de Busbecq, put it this way: "As for the site of the city itself, it seems to have been created by nature for the capital of the world. . . .

No place could be more beautiful or more conveniently situated." The sultans set out to make it even more grand.

Over time, the city began to hold the sultans. It was easier to live in a beautiful place than sleep in tents in dangerous territory. Sultans used to send their sons out to the provinces to learn imperial administration and war. How could that compare to good times with poets, and luxury in the city? Even the Janissaries, the elite soldiers, began to settle down, taking wives and doing crafts to supplement their income. Turks and other Muslims might make up a majority of the population of the empire, but in Istanbul they were barely more than half, and many of the officials were former European *devshirme* boys originally from Europe.

SULEYMAN ELUDES THE POISONED SHIRT

Suleyman the Magnificent, the sultan of the Ottoman Empire from 1520 to 1566, made the capital even more beautiful. The Venetian ambassador Bartolomeo Cantavini described Suleyman as "tall, but thin with a delicate complexion. His nose is too long, his features fine. . . . His general appearance is pleasing." In some ways, he was a ruler like the sultans before him, a successful military leader who died on his last campaign when he was 70. He was also a unique individual, part warrior, part poet. Suleyman was capable of writing very matter-of-factly about terrible events, some he himself had caused. After the Battle of Mohacs in Hungary, he wrote a diary in the third person, "The Sultan seated on a golden throne, receives the homage of the viziers and beys [officials]; massacre of 2,000 prisoners; the rain falls in torrents." On the other hand, he fell so in love with Roxelana, a Russian or Ukrainian slave, that he broke tradition and, surprising everyone, married her. His love letters to her are quite different from his diary entries. Roxelana was to him "the green of my garden, my sweet sugar, my treasure, my love who cares for nothing in this world."

Suleyman the Magnificent believed that frequent hunting trips kept sultans in fighting form. He commented in a letter to King Francis I of France, "Day and night our horse is saddled and our sword is girded."

The love he had for Roxelana, and hers for him, must have been a relief after his childhood with his father, known as Selim the Grim. Although Suleyman respected his father

Flowers of cobalt and turquoise blue, typical of fine pottery from Damascus, Syria, decorate a foot basin that Suleyman probably found very useful after long, hot days during military campaigns. Pottery designs like this originated in China, but the Ottomans began to produce their own for Silk Road trade.

for adding much territory to the empire, defeating the Mamluks in Egypt in 1516, and taking over the pilgrimage routes to Mecca and Medina, there was little affection between father and son. Selim sent Suleyman into the provinces to learn administration, and the two rarely saw each other. According to court stories, Selim, fearing his son's popularity, sent him a poisoned shirt. Suleyman's mother, Hafisa Khatoun, a Tartar and descendant of Genghis Khan, became suspicious of this sudden gift and told a slave put it on. The slave died and so, shortly after, did Selim. Chance? Perhaps not.

Suleyman was his father's son when it came to adding territory to the empire. At the Battle of Mohacs in 1526 his army fought allied troops from Hungary, Poland, Germany, and Bohemia (currently the Czech Republic). The young king of Hungary, Louis, was in charge of the battle. Some of his older advisers wanted him to pull back to Budapest so that Turkish supply lines would be lengthened and easier to attack. But the Hungarian knights were eager to fight and wanted to win before other allies showed up to share the glory in winning. The Hungarians charged straight into the center of the Turkish line, and in a fierce fight reached Suleyman and shot at him. The superior Turkish artillery fired at the Hungarians, however, and the battlefield at Mohacs became known as "the tomb of the Hungarian nation." Suleyman's September 2 diary entry records "rest at Mohacs, 20,000 Hungarian infantry and 7,000 of their cavalry are buried."

After taking over Hungary and thus becoming a major European power, Suleyman tried to extend his empire. The Ottoman victory over Christian crusaders called the St.

"The most memorable and lofty occasion which past centuries have beheld, nor do those to come hope to see the like."

—Spanish writer Miguel de Cervantes
describing the Battle of Lepanto, *Exemplary Novels*, 1613

John Hospitallers Knights at the Greek island of Rhodes opened up the eastern Mediterranean to their navy. There were also some defeats. South of Italy, the island nation of Malta resisted attack, and Suleyman's attempt to take Vienna in 1529 failed as an early winter set in. The problem with attacking central Europe for the sultans was a short fighting season. By the time they left Istanbul in April or May, were forced to march to Vienna or Budapest and maintain a long siege, the weather would be turning cold. Since the Turks sometimes brought as many as 100,000 horses with them, finding proper fodder when snow began to fall was a problem. Moving the capital further north might have worked, but then the trip for Turkish troops back to Anatolia would have been too far. The empire was beginning to reach the limit of Ottoman military ability.

Poised outside the walls of Vienna in 1529, Suleyman's Ottoman commanders mount an ultimately unsuccessful attack on the city. Unusually heavy rains slowed down the Ottomans long enough for the Europeans to send a joint Catholic and Protestant force to the city's aid.

Suleyman saw himself as a man of order as well as a warrior. In Ottoman sources he is usually referred to as Suleyman the Law-Giver. One of the tasks he set for his reign was the creation of a legal system, bringing it up to date. These laws touched all parts of Ottoman life, including how much butter should be placed in pastry or how large a fine a man must pay for stealing a kiss from an unwilling woman. The purpose of the Kanun-i-Osman, the laws, was to prevent the "committing of acts of injustice" throughout the growing empire.

Suleyman gained his nickname "Magnificent" partly because he encouraged the arts, which flourished during his reign. He surrounded himself with poets, such as Baki, whom he called the "king of the poets," and Hayali, who went with him on a Baghdad campaign. He supported a group of visual artists, some of whom experimented with Western styles. The miniatures of Addul Celil

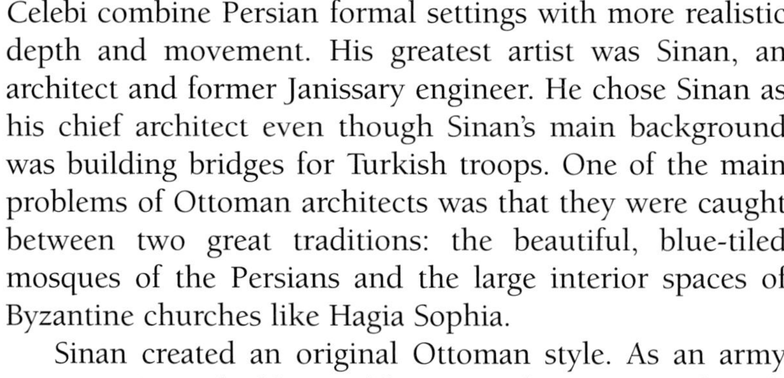

Celebi combine Persian formal settings with more realistic depth and movement. His greatest artist was Sinan, an architect and former Janissary engineer. He chose Sinan as his chief architect even though Sinan's main background was building bridges for Turkish troops. One of the main problems of Ottoman architects was that they were caught between two great traditions: the beautiful, blue-tiled mosques of the Persians and the large interior spaces of Byzantine churches like Hagia Sophia.

Selimiye Mosque in Edirne, Turkey, is a celebration of circles, with a great central space, half-circle windows and decorative wheels of colors on the round dome. The spoils from the Ottoman victory in Cyprus in 1569 provided funds for the building, which the architect, Sinan, considered his best work.

Sinan created an original Ottoman style. As an army engineer, Sinan had learned how to order troops and work quickly under pressure. Using these skills, he designed a remarkable number of buildings. One was the Suleymaniye mosque complex in Istanbul, built to celebrate Suleyman's victories. Its high minarets (slender towers attached to a mosque); the choice of a site overlooking the city and sea; and the grouping of a mosque, hospital, school, and dormitories makes it one of the world's most photographed buildings. The Ottomans now "owned" the skyline of Istanbul. For Sinan, however, his Mosque of Selimiye in Edirne, on the border with Greece, was his masterpiece, with a very complicated design of colored stone. Sinan's buildings try to match Hagia Sophia's huge interior spaces while still using the minarets to point to God's vast spaces beyond.

With all his achievements and those of his talented artists, Suleyman still faced the Ottoman dilemma of succession. When his favorite son died, he had to choose among his remaining sons one to train for the sultanate. Not surprisingly, his choice went to Roxelana's sons, even though another son, Mustafa, from a different mother, was more talented. On his father's orders, palace guards strangled Mustafa, which did not eliminate the rivalry between Roxelana's sons. Before her death, according to Ambassador de Busbecq, Roxelana thought her son Beyazit was best, but Selim was Suleyman's choice—and an unfortunate one. A drunkard, he became known as Selim the Sot. Some historians criticize Roxelana's influence for the killing of Mustafa and cite Selim as the beginning of the decline of the Ottomans. However, the empire had survived poor rulers before, and other forces began to limit Ottoman expansion.

"I cannot deny that I very much want to see the Turk powerful and ready for war, not for his own sake, for he is an infidel and the rest of us are Christians, but to erode the power of the Emperor [Charles V] and involve him in crippling expenses."

—Francis I of France, writing to the Venetian ambassador, 1536

SPRING TULIPS, WILTING EMPIRE

After Suleyman's death in 1566, no sultans regularly went on military campaigns. One reason was that after 1590, no sultan had any military training. Later sultans removed the law of fratricide; no longer would the sultan automatically kill his brothers to ensure his rule. Instead, princes would be placed in the Cage, a limited area of the palace. There they would be well treated and live in luxury with concubines, but would have no freedom to leave. Instead of training in the provinces or being part of long military marches, the princes knew little of the outside world. Even their mothers, confined to the harem, had once seen more of the world in their lives before slavery. One sultan, brought suddenly to the throne, had spent the first 40 years of his life in the Cage.

For the Janissaries, this lack of able leadership became a problem. They staged revolts to get rid of some of the worst sultans, such as Ibrahim, nicknamed the Mad. Settled into life in Constantinople with their families, the Janissaries began bringing their sons into the army, whether they had talent or not. The Janissaries refused to listen seriously to the foreign advisers brought in to teach the new musket tactics that the Europeans were developing. Worse yet for the Ottomans, their military was beginning to face serious defeats, both on sea and land.

The Battle of Lepanto in 1571 was a naval contest in which the Habsburg Empire of central Europe beat the

Camel Train to Mecca

ANONYMOUS, ARCHIVES OF THE TURKISH PRIME MINISTER, 1749

After Selim I took Egypt and Syria, the Ottomans had the honor, but also the responsibility, of guarding religious pilgrimages to the holy city of Mecca. This was no easy task, as the pilgrims needed 152 days to journey just from Damascus to Mecca and back. This pilgrimage, called the Haj, was an obligation for Muslims. In some years, only a third of the pilgrims would survive the hardships of the journey that included bandit attacks. Seven months before the pilgrims would leave Damascus, they had to draw up a budget. This document is one such written estimate submitted to the Ottoman state treasurer in 1749 for the needed funding.

To ensure the safe departure and return, with God's help of the joyful pilgrims who will travel in 1749 on the Damascus pilgrimage route under the supervision of the present governor of Damascus and commander of the pilgrimage, Hacci Esat Pasha, the following expenses are recorded: wages and extras for 1,500 mercenary [paid] foot soldiers and cavalrymen, camels and other expenses, rental of camels for 400 Damascus local troops, basic and supplementary payments to Arab tribes [bribes to keep them from raiding]. . . . Accordingly, upon your excellency's approval, these will be recorded in the chief comptroller's office and the necessary certificates, copies, and orders pertaining to the stated sums will be written. Orders to proceed are requested from your excellency.

Muslims, on foot and mounted on horses and camels, make their way to Mecca on the Haj, a holy journey of worship. From 1517 to 1917, the Ottomans protected the route, known as the Imperial Way, from bandits.

Turkish fleet. As one of the Turkish documents of the time explained: "The Imperial fleet encountered the fleet of the wretched infidels and the will of God turned another way." The Turks suffered heavy losses, perhaps as many as 30,000 men. The Europeans freed 15,000 Christian galley slaves who had been chained as rowers for the Turkish fleet. The Turks had the resources to rebuild their fleet, which they did fairly quickly. As a grand vizier put it, "The might of the empire is such that if it were desired to equip the entire fleet with silver anchors, silken riggings and satin sails, we could do it." The real question was whether the new navy would give up galley ships and develop new designs for fast-moving ships relying on sails and well-trained captains, as the Europeans were doing.

Janissary officers wore elaborate costumes and headdresses. Feathers or metal strips called celeng *were awarded for bravery in war. A green turban was reserved for high officials and descendants of the prophet Muhammad.*

The battle ending the siege of Vienna in 1683 also shocked the Turks. Mehmet IV had sent General Kara Mustafa with 100,000 troops to take Vienna, capital of the Habsburg Empire. Instead of the innovative, try-anything tactics Mehmet II had used in taking Constantinople, Kara Mustafa settled into a siege to starve out the Viennese. Some of the Janissaries muttered that Kara Mustafa wanted the Austrians to give in, meaning that the commander would get a percentage of the loot from the city. If the city was taken by force, the Janissaries would have three days of rioting, destroying, and looting—and Kara Mustafa would lose money. Whatever his reasoning, Mustafa waited, and the siege went on long enough for Europeans to put together a major force.

The French duke of Lorraine and the Polish king Jan Sobieski attacked with their troops. Focused on the walls of Vienna, Kara Mustafa had not protected the perimeter of his forces. The result was a drive by the Europeans that pushed through the thin outlying defenses all the way to the walls of the city. Sobieski's forces captured Mustafa's tent and

> *"I live in a place that very well represents the Tower of Babel; in Pera [a suburb of Constantinople] they speak Turkish, Greek, Hebrew, Armenian, Arabic, Persian, Russian, Slavonian, Wallachian, German, Dutch, French English, Italian, and what is worse, there is ten of these languages spoken in my own family. . . I live in the perpetual hearing of this medley of sounds, which produces a very extraordinary effect upon the people who live here."*
>
> —Lady Mary Wortley Montagu, wife of the English ambassador to the Turkish court, letter, March 10, 1718

equipment; the Ottoman leader's jeweled stirrup was sent to Poland as a message of victory. Kara Mustafa had 50 of his pashas (leaders) executed to shift blame for the defeat. On his way back to Istanbul, he himself was strangled on an order from the sultan.

There were other defeats, as Serbia, Hungary, parts of Persia, the North African sultanates, and others areas broke away from the empire. In 1686, when Christians retook the city of Buda in Hungary, a soldier's song showed Muslim despair:

> In the mosques there is no more prayer.
> In the fountains no more ablution [washing].
> The populous places have become desolate.
> The Austrian has taken our beautiful Buda.

The drive and will to retake these places seemed beyond the abilities of some of the sultans. Perhaps they were war weary. Ahmet III was bored and upset with life in the palace. As he wrote in a letter to the grand vizier, "I go out to one of the chambers [large rooms]. Forty chamber members line up. It is never comfortable." Ahmet III, instead, started the less formal Tulip Era from 1703 to 1730, a period in which he tried to combine Ottoman and European cultures.

The Ottoman government had sent ambassadors to France, and they came back with drawings of French palaces such as the elaborate Fontainebleau. Ahmet was so impressed that he built a replica, Sa'adabad Palace, away from all those dreary chamber members. At Sa'adabad, he had gardens planted with thousands of tulips. Like many Europeans, he gave in to the tulip mania of the era, which transformed the flower into a symbol of wealth. A special Festival of Spring, started in 1708, was held in Ahmet's gardens. Visitors were told what colors to wear to match the tulips, and specially colored lamps flickered before mirrors at night. What seemed to strike visitors most were the small candles placed on the backs of turtles creeping slowly among the tulips in the evening.

Ahmet III also surrounded himself with poets who appreciated the life of relaxation and beauty he was creating

The immense Blue Mosque in Istanbul created controversy in the Islamic world as it was being built. Not only had Ahmet I failed to win any battles to pay for construction, its six minarets rivaled the more important mosque at Mecca, which had only one more.

in Istanbul. The poet Nedim described this life to a friend in his poem:

> Let us laugh, let us play and take pleasure from the world!
> Let us drink and waters that the springs of Eden bring!
> . . . Let us go to Sa'adabad, my moving cypress tree.

Sir Robert Sutton, the English ambassador to the Ottomans at the time, reported that, "The Turks grow weary of war." In his own rather playboy way, however, Ahmet III was showing that Europeans had something to offer the Ottomans. He allowed the first printing press for Turkish books, supported the publication of Turkish works, and

"Raise high thy voice like David of the Psalms, What e're remains, under the dome, is but some pleasant sound."

—Poet Baki, an elegy for Suleyman the Magnificent, 1566

built a large library. Like other sultans, he tried to bring in Europeans to modernize the army.

The Muslim judges, known as the Ulema and the Janissaries had other ideas. They saw technologies like the printing press as the dangerous "novelties" and "innovations" that the Quran, the Islamic holy book, warned against. The Janissaries also resisted change and their leaders led a revolt against Ahmet III. Bloodshed ended the Tulip Era: the pleasure palace of Sa'adabad was destroyed; Ahmet had to agree to the killing of his advisors; and the poet Nedim was chased over rooftops until he fell to his death.

Mahmud I, Ahmet's successor, acted as if he went along with the rebels, but later invited the Janissary leaders to the palace, where he had them killed. Mahmud kept the library and pushed quietly for change. In the years that followed the Tulip Era, various sultans worked for reform, even abolishing the Janissaries in 1826. The tension between keeping a proud Ottoman heritage in the midst of increased Western technology and power continued to haunt Ottoman leaders. In 1707, during the brief Tulip Era, Ibrahim Muteferrika, a Hungarian convert to Islam, published a book, *Rational Bases for the Politics of Nation.* He raised this question, "Why do Christian nations which were so weak in the past compared with Muslim nations begin to dominate many lands in modern times and even defeat the once victorious Ottoman armies?" As the 18th century proceeded, not only the Ottomans would be disturbed by that question.

CHAPTER 8

STOCKING THE ROYAL SPICE CABINET

THE PORTUGUESE EMPIRE

Sometimes buildings reveal a nation's history. Three of Portugal's major buildings are the Batalha Monastery, the Belem Tower, and the Hieryonimites Monastery. Each tells part of the story of Portugal's rise as a great naval power and as the first nation to sail its own ships into ports in Japan, China, Malaysia, India, South Africa, and Brazil. Portugal's burst of exploration was remarkable for any nation, and especially so for a poor, small country. Two-thirds of Portugal's soil was too rocky for cultivation; its rivers were not easily navigated, and unpredictable rainfall made growing crops difficult. Only in 1249 had Portugal, with the aid of crusaders on their way to the Holy Land, been able to push out the Muslim Arabs who had controlled much of the country since 711. Even then, neighboring Spanish states tried to gain control of Portugal. The first Portuguese monarch to rule independent of Spain was Afonso Henrique, who came to the throne in 1143. Yet, in little more than a century after Portugal gained the same

Belem Tower sits at the mouth of the Tagus River, controlling the entrance into Lisbon's harbor. Attempting to describe how sailors might feel as they passed the tower on their way to the sea, the poet Luis de Camoes wrote: "The people considered us already lost, On so long and uncertain a journey, the women with piteous wailing. . . "

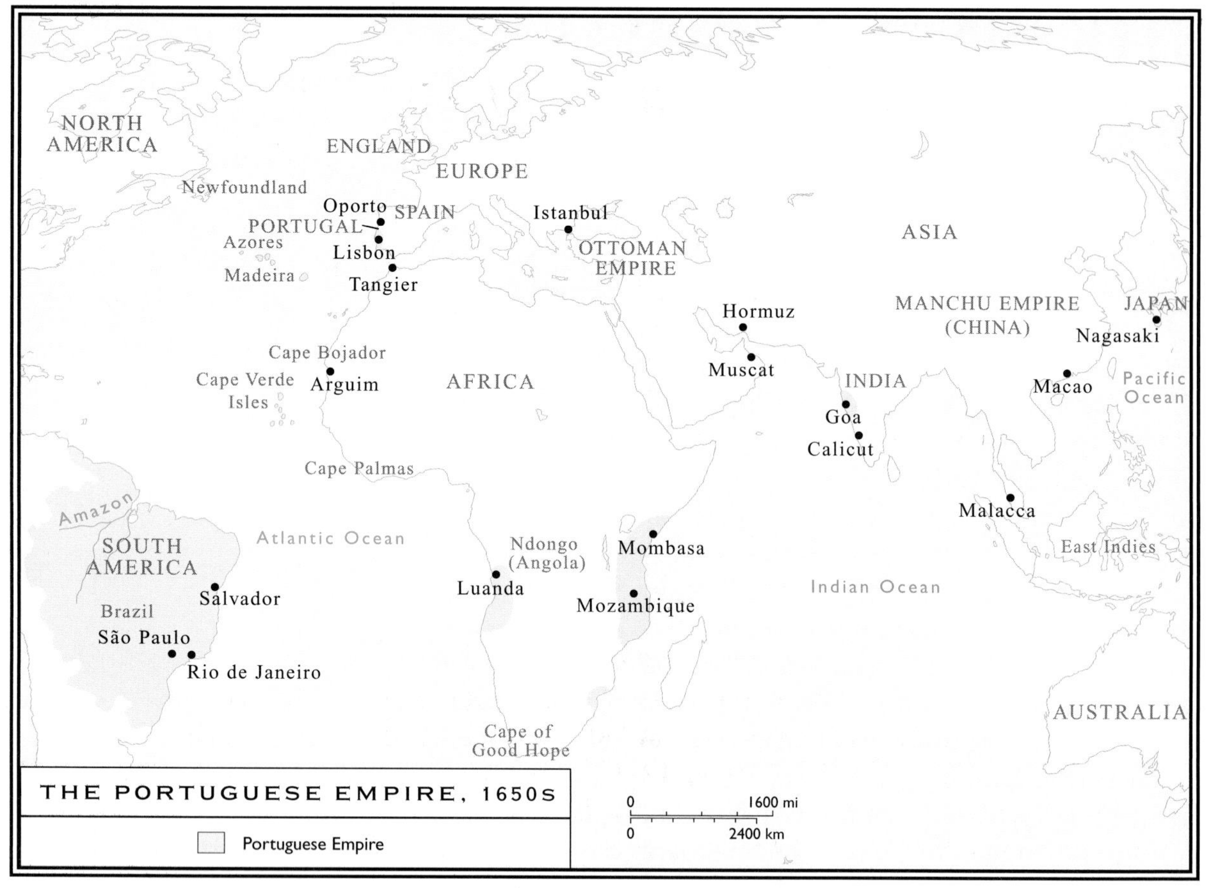

boundaries it has today, the Portuguese began venturing out into the rest of the world.

The empire they built as a result of the exploration was, as one historian put it, like a meteor, coming unexpectedly. Much of what they gained in colonial wealth was later lost, but the changes the empire brought—from new foods to terrible slavery to religious strife—were significant. The stones of Portugal's buildings are also part of that history.

The Batalha Monastery is a huge church in a very small town, A Batalha, which means "the battle." The building celebrates the Portuguese victory over Spanish troops at the Battle of Aljubarrota on August 14, 1385. This was a conflict between Joao and Beatrice, the son and daughter of the deceased Portuguese king, for the crown of Portugal. Joao had the advantage that the Portuguese liked him, he was a good warrior, and he was married to Philippa of England. Her English archers would join his forces. His disadvantage was that he was an illegitimate son. Beatrice's main claim was that she was legitimate, the king's recognized daughter. Further, as the wife of the king of the largest Spanish state, Castile, she could unite Portugal with it. The night before the fighting began, Joao promised the Virgin Mary that he would build a church for her if he won. The next day, Joao's troops took the high ground at Aljubarrota, waited for Beatrice's Castilian troops to attack, and with English arrows flying, killed many of the knights charging against them.

The Batalha Monastery is the result of Joao's promise, but it reveals another aspect of Portuguese history as well, namely exploration. It is the tomb of Joao and Philippa's son, Prince Henry the Navigator, the leader of Portuguese exploration. He had asked to be buried near his parents so he could serve them after death as he had served them in life. This sense of duty was one of the leading characteristics of Henry's personality. Unmarried, he was a member of several Christian crusading orders and managed the earliest Portuguese sea explorations down the coast of Africa. The inscription on his tomb bears the words *talant de bienfere*, meaning "a hunger to perform great deeds."

HENRY, ARMCHAIR NAVIGATOR

Though statues of Henry the Navigator are found throughout Portugal, the main modern symbol for him is the Monument to Discoveries, a large structure in Lisbon near the Belem Tower. The Belem Tower itself is a stone fortress, built in 1515 to guard the entry into Lisbon. In the early 1500s it was the last sight of Portugal for sailors on their way out to sea. A Jesuit priest, Antonio Vierira, wrote in the 1600s that "God gave the Portuguese a small country as a cradle, but the world as their grave." Many Portuguese explorers, such as Ferdinand Magellan and thousands of

The Portuguese Monument to the Discoveries, built in 1960 to remember the 500th anniversary of Prince Henry the Navigator's death, shows him as if on the prow of a ship. On either side of the monument are sculptures of people who supported exploration, including King Manuel I, author Luis de Camoes, and Henry's mother, Philippa of England.

others, were lost at sea or killed in distant lands. Between 1700 and 1730, some 25,000 died in the Portuguese Royal Hospital in Goa, India, of disease and wounds. The explorer Vasco da Gama's fleet of 1498 limped home with only one-third of its men. Other fleets never returned.

Portuguese sailors probably reached the fishing banks off Newfoundland, Canada, in the early 1400s, but kept their plentiful catches of halibut and cod secret. They tried, unsuccessfully, to claim Newfoundland in 1510. To the west, Portuguese sailors took over Madeira, an island in the North Atlantic, in 1419, and Brazil in 1500. To the south, Portuguese sails rounded Africa in 1488 and moved on to the east, reaching India in 1498.

When folded, this navigational instrument, called a compendium, could fit easily in a ship captain's pocket. The seven layers contained a sundial for keeping time, a table with the locations of major European ports, and a perpetual calendar for keeping track of the date as well as religious holidays.

Though several monarchs sponsored and many sailors participated in these voyages, Henry the Navigator went to exceptional lengths to make them happen. He gathered around him a group of mapmakers and men willing to take risks. Exploration down the West African coast, beginning in 1415, went slowly. Beyond Cape Bojador off the coast of Africa below Morocco, according to captured Muslim informants, lay only "the Green Sea of Darkness" and monsters. Southeast trade winds pushed against ships, making voyages lengthy and costly. Though the Portuguese took some slaves and traded for some gold on these voyages, expenses outweighed their profits. It took 15 attempts before Gil Eanes, a Portuguese explorer, rounded the dreaded Cape Bojador in 1484 and found no darkness, no monsters.

The Portuguese had developed a ship, the caravel, that had a lateen, or triangular, sail slanted sideways to catch slight breezes and a low draft (or hull) to get into the shallow African coastline. Being low to the water, the ship was also vulnerable to attack, and Africans defended themselves with poison arrows. As one Portuguese captain told Prince Henry's chronicler Gomes Eanes Zurara: "They [the Africans] are not as easy to capture as he [Zurara] thought for, believe me, they are very strong and skillful in defending themselves." The Portuguese would later work with African chiefs to buy slaves rather than trying to capture them.

Slavery, however, was not the main purpose of these voyages south. The Ottomans had conquered Constantinople and therefore controlled the major spice routes to the East. Henry pushed to find an alternate route. Bartolomeu Dias, a Portuguese navigator and explorer, set out with three ships in 1487 and finally rounded the cape of southern Africa in 1488. Ironically, a fog had settled in and he had to wait for the return trip to actually see the cape. According to some sources, Dias named the tip of Africa the Cape of Storms, a sailor's view of the weather, and a fitting name, as Dias himself later died there. The Portuguese ruler, thinking perhaps of the riches of India, renamed it the Cape of Good Hope.

Now that Dias had proven there was a navigable route around Africa, the Portuguese king Manuel I outfitted the explorer Vasco da Gama with four ships carrying 170 men in 1498. The main goals of da Gama's trip were to increase Portugal's wealth through trade or conquest, expand the realm of Christianity by continuing the crusader tradition, and find a mysterious Christian kingdom said to be in the East. As one of da Gama's men replied when asked why they had come to India, "We have come to seek Christians and spices." Everyone understood about spices. Europeans needed them to enhance boring meals or mask the taste of unrefrigerated, rotting foods. Because most of these spices—pepper, cinnamon, mace, nutmeg—came from Southeast Asia to Europe over long land and sea routes controlled by Muslims, the cost was very high. Successfully delivering one shipload of spices allowed a captain to retire for life—after giving a substantial cut of his profit to the king, of course.

Vasco da Gama was an excellent choice to command the first European voyage to India in search of all those spices. He stubbornly fought the trade winds, the usual weather patterns, south along Africa, swinging far out into the Atlantic, then rounding the Cape of Good Hope. His total voyage lasted four times as long as Columbus's trip to America and covered 27,000 miles. Despite scurvy among his sailors; being out of sight of land for long periods; and

"Thus went we opening those seas,
which save Our own no Nation open'd ere before,
Seeing those new Isles and climates near which brave Prince Henry shewd unto the world before."

—Poet Luis de Camoes describing Portuguese exploration, *The Luciads*, 1572

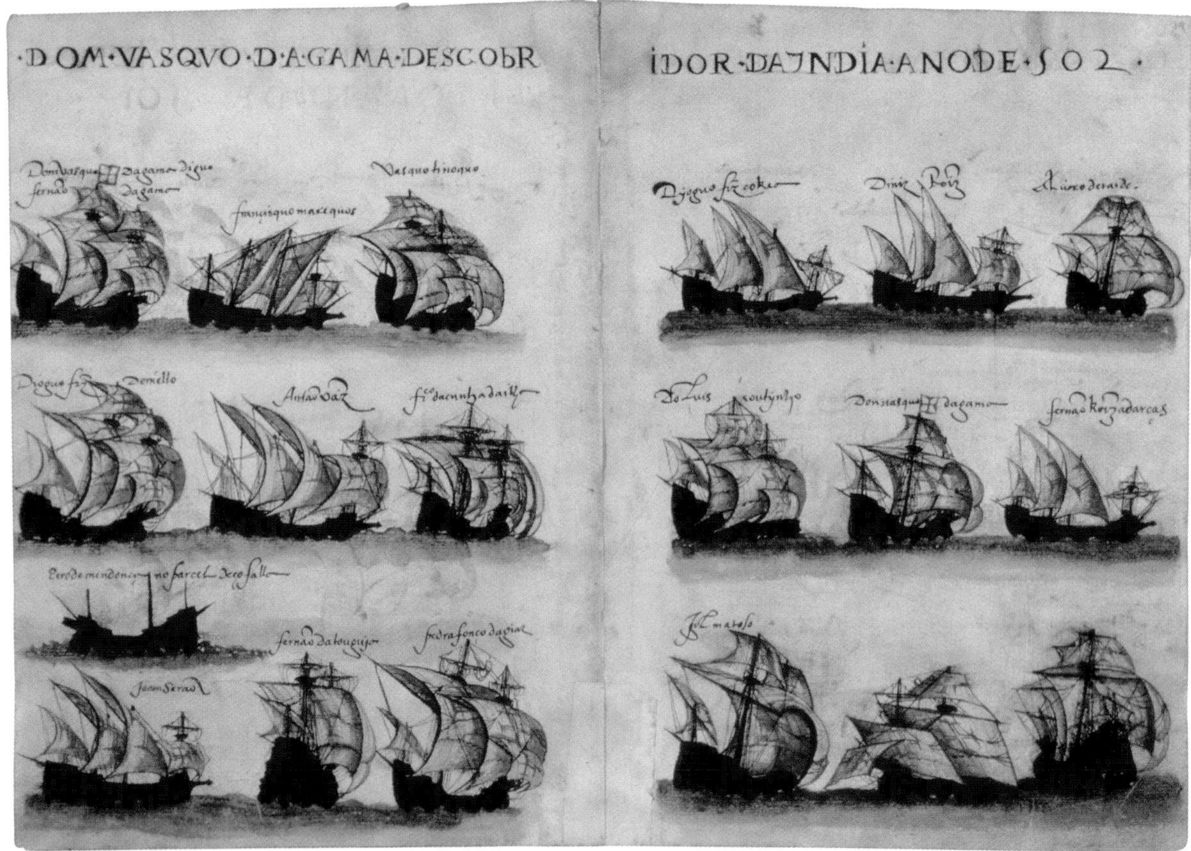

Hoping to reach the spices of India by sailing around the tip of southern Africa, Vasco da Gama's fleet started out on July 8, 1497. This voyage led so many others to follow his example that, in the words of the Portuguese poet Sado Mirand, "At the scent of cinnamon, the kingdom loses its people."

being threatened by Africans, Muslims, and Hindus in a variety of settings, he did make it back to Portugal, although with few spices. Indian rulers laughed at the paltry goods he had brought to trade and insisted on gold. But he courageously stood up to an Indian ruler who had trapped his ships in a harbor. Later as admiral of the fleet, he revealed a cruel side. He ordered his men to burn an Arab ship with women and children on board that came too close to him.

Other Portuguese continued what da Gama had begun. Afonso de Albuquerque, an officer in the king's navy, used larger Portuguese ships, galleons with mounted guns, to establish a network of fortified cities for trade: the Indian city Goa (1510), the Malaysian city of Malacca (1511), the Persian city of Hormuz (1515), and the Chinese city of Macau (1557). He claimed that an empire could be held "with four good fortresses and a large well-armed fleet manned by 3,000 European born Portuguese." The Portuguese also found, as they had in Africa, that they needed only to control outposts, not the interior, for trading. So in Southeast Asia, Macau in China, and Nagasaki in Japan, they set up "factories," trading centers with ports, warehouses, and administrators. They also brought Roman Catholic priests who attempted, with varying success, to convert the local people to Christianity.

In Brazil, however, there were more than just outposts. In 1500, a fleet of 13 ships commanded by the Portuguese navigator Pedro Alvares Cabral made the wide sweep to catch the trade winds to round the Cape of Good Hope, but then sighted the Brazilian coast. Brazil would offer much to Portugal; its sugar fields, worked first by exploited natives, and later by slaves brought from Africa, produced high-grade sugar popular in Europe. American Indians were pushed back from their lands. The Portuguese discovered silver there in 1545, then gold and diamonds—all flowing into the treasuries of the kings of Portugal and out again to pay for weapons and commerce with the rest of Europe.

The Hieryonimites Monastery in Lisbon serves as an ideal example of much of this early, lavish time. Its architectural

Native Americans in feathered headdresses, macaws (tropical birds), monkeys, and reptiles crowd a 1519 Portuguese map of Brazil. The vastness of Brazil led the missionary Francisco Pires to complain in 1552, "At times a year goes by and we know nothing of one another and the few ships that go up and down the coast."

style is called Manueline after King Manuel I, who with all the American wealth coming in, was nicknamed the Fortunate. The monastery is intricately decorated inside and out, with Muslim, Renaissance, Baroque and Gothic styles; the king loved them all. Manuel built the monastery itself to celebrate Vasco da Gama's voyage to India, and the wealth of the spice trade helped to finance the construction. Da Gama's tomb is there; his body was brought back from Goa, India, where he died in 1524. Fittingly, some of the high stone columns of the church are carved to look like the rope riggings on his ships, and the columns themselves give the illusion of ship masts.

Across the aisle from da Gama's tomb is that of Luis de Camoes, who also spent time in Goa, though he was exiled there for rowdiness and fighting his fellow soldiers. Camoes illustrates another side of Portuguese exploration; often criminals were released to help fill shortages of colonial troops or sailors. His honored place across from da Gama has less to do with his somewhat shady career than with the poetry he wrote. His epic poem *The Luciads* tells the

The elaborate combination of spires, arches, and sculptures in Lisbon's Hieryonimites Monastery reflect the wealth that poured into Portugal during the early days of its empire. Charles Frederic de Merveilleaus, a visiting Swiss soldier, wrote of Portuguese palaces and churches: "It is certain that three quarters of the King's treasury and of the gold brought [from] Brazil were... changed to stone."

story of Portugal's struggle to "track the oceans none had sailed before," as he put it. So central to Portuguese history and literature is Camoes that the date of his death, June 10, is commemorated as the celebration day of the Portuguese people.

Another Portuguese hero, King Sebastian, is remembered in the Hieryonimites Monastery in Lisbon with a symbolic tomb showing human figures from various parts of the Portuguese Empire. Sebastian, like Prince Henry, never married, and considered himself a crusader. Presumably killed in an attack on Muslim territory in North Africa—his body was never recovered—Sebastian became a sort of King Arthur figure in Portuguese history, someone who might yet return to save his country. After Sebastian's death, the closest heir to the Portuguese throne was King Philip II of Spain. Philip used his army and bribes to the Portuguese nobility to win the Portuguese throne. As Philip put it, "I inherited it; I bought it and I conquered it." Many Portuguese hated Spanish domination and held out hope that somehow, Sebastian might return. The Portuguese refer to this era of Spanish domination as "the Spanish Captivity."

RUNNING OUT OF WIND

The Spanish brought the Inquisition, a court set up to investigate religious beliefs, to Portugal and gave Portuguese Jews the choice of leaving or converting. Even if they converted to Christianity, Jews were harassed; 36,000 cases were brought to the Inquisition, and 1,500 people were burned at the stake. The Inquisition spread to the Portuguese colonies. At Goa, for example, Hindus wondered why widow burning, which was traditional in their culture, was outlawed when the burning of the "New Christians" was so frequent. A French traveler, François Pyrard, who visited Goa from 1608 to 1610, described the atmosphere there: "For the least suspicion, the slightest word, whether of a child or of a slave who wishes to do his master a bad turn, is enough to hang a man."

Spanish rule also brought Portugal into direct confrontation with the English and the Dutch. After Philip II

The Longest Journey

GOMES EANNES DE ZURARA, CHRONICLE OF THE DISCOVERY AND CONQUEST OF GUINEA, 15TH CENTURY

Prince Henry of Portugal was a contradictory person. Though he is called the Navigator, he was not a sailor, and the North African coast was as far as he actually went by sea. But he was the instigator of Portuguese voyages and paid many of their costs, winding up in debt. The following account is from a book by Gomes Eannes de Zurara, a chronicler at Henry's court, and for the most part, an admirer of Henry's career. However, in his description of the first slaves brought to Henry from one of these voyages in 1444, Zurara makes clear his sympathy for the slaves and revulsion at the slave auction. Henry watched, took his royal portion, one-fifth of the slaves, and gave thanks he was saving so many for God.

Neither an explorer nor a navigator, Prince Henry directed and financed many of the voyages that expanded the Portuguese empire.

What heart could be so hard, as not to be pierced with piteous feeling to see that company? For some kept their heads low, and their face bathed in tears, looking one upon another. Others stood groaning very dolorously [sadly], looking up to the height of heaven, fixing their eyes upon it, crying out loudly, as if asking help from the Father of nature; others struck their faces with the palms of their hands, throwing themselves full length upon the ground; while others made lamentations in the manner of a dirge, after the custom of their country. . . .

But to increase their sufferings still more, there now arrived those who had charge of the division of the captives, and . . . then was it needful to part fathers from sons, husbands from wives, brothers from brothers. No respect was shown to either friends nor relations, but each fell where his lot took him. . . .

Oh, mighty Fortune, who, with thy wheel doest and undoest, compassing the matters of the world as it pleaseth thee, do thou at least put before the eyes of that miserable race some understanding of matters to come, that the captives may receive some consolation in the midst of their great sorrow.

> *"The discovery of America and that of a passage to the East Indies by the Cape of Good Hope are the two greatest and most important events recorded in the history of mankind."*
>
> —Scottish economist Adam Smith, *The Wealth of Nations*, 1776

claimed the throne of England, the Portuguese were included in Philip's plans for the Spanish fleet to invade England. Hundreds of Portuguese sailors and dozens of ships were lost as heavy seas and the English Navy destroyed the Spanish Armada in 1588. Spain's brutality against inhabitants of the Netherlands also rebounded on the Portuguese. Once the Dutch had thrown out the Spanish and established their independence, they used their fast, well-armed ships and better-trained captains to attack Portugal's trading places in Asia, Brazil, and Africa. Though Portugal retained some places, like Goa, Brazil, Macau, and the African country of Angola, the Dutch East India Company took over the rich spice trade.

In 1668, Portugal managed, through insurrections, to reestablish its independence. Sugar, gold, and diamonds still brought some wealth from Brazil. Its kings frittered away much, not on roads or education to develop Portugal or its colonies, but instead on buildings like the palace at Mafra, a city in Portugal, which needed the labor of 48,000 workers to build 800 rooms and 5,200 doorways. By the late 1700s, Portugal still had no well-respected, modern university.

There were many who felt little sorrow at the dwindling of the Portuguese Empire. Portugal had started the transatlantic slave trade that had, in some periods, brought as many as 10,000 slaves a year to Brazil. Though brave Africans such as Queen Nzinga of Ndongo (now Angola) fought, in 1626, to limit Portuguese slavery, estimates are that the Portuguese brought 4 million African slaves to South America. The American Indians, faced with newly introduced diseases such as smallpox and Portuguese violence, suffered as well. Today there are 270,000 native

Ships crowd Lisbon's harbor in the mid-16th century as Portugal becomes the first European power to face two great world wind systems, the Atlantic trade winds and the monsoons of the Indian Ocean. At the height of its empire Portugal had a fleet of 300 ocean-going ships.

people in Brazil; in 1500 there were millions. In a letter to Portuguese officials, the Jesuit priest Fernao Cardim described the "assaults, robberies, captivities and other vexations that always were done to [the Indians], and even now are done. Against the Indians was always a rigorous justice; they have already been hanged, hewn in pieces, quartered." Justice, the priest felt, "will come from Heaven on all the inhabitants of Brazil" for the crimes against the American Indians.

By 1750, Portugal had to face a future in which it could no longer depend on outside wealth to prop up its economy. An earthquake and devastating fire in Lisbon in 1757 only added to Portugal's woes. As the Portuguese battled poverty and political instability at home they held on to fragments of their empire into the late 20th century. The wealth of the past empire might have done so much to prepare Portugal for more modern times, but that was gone. The buildings—Batalha, Belem Tower, and Hieryonimites—still stood.

CHAPTER 9

"GO FURTHER!"

SPAIN EXPANDS ACROSS AN OCEAN

"Have Empire, Will Travel" would have been a good motto to put on Spain's coat of arms in the era from 1400 to 1700. Isabella of Castile, one of the founders of the empire, traveled so much throughout Spain that she was known as "the queen on horseback." To gain control of Spain's crusaders for Ferdinand, her husband, king of Aragon, she rode three days, all day, to reach the arranged meeting place. Before the Battle of Zubia against the Moors, she put on armor, as her childhood hero Joan of Arc had done, and rode through a rugged mountain pass to inspire her troops. The marriage of Isabella and Ferdinand joined the regions of Spain that they ruled over, Castile and Aragon, and they intended to unite all of Spain with their travels by gaining support from local lords. As they went through towns and villages, they kept notebooks of the talented people they met. Trying not to rely on powerful landowning nobles who had created a fractured Spain with their rivalries and petty wars, Ferdinand and Isabella wanted a wider network of advisers, loyal primarily to them. They had no real capital city; the saddle, the saying went, was the throne of Spain.

Queen Isabella of Castile and King Ferdinand II of Aragon triumphantly enter Granada with their troops after the Moors surrender in 1492. The English essayist Francis Bacon wrote that their reign was "the cornerstone of the greatness of Spain that followed."

Their grandson, Charles V, had even more territory to travel. When he became king in 1516, he inherited not only Spain but also much of Italy and the Netherlands. In addition, he was elected Holy Roman Emperor, leader of the German states. His motto, "Go Further," certainly describes his travels. "Kings," Charles V wrote in a letter to his son Philip, "do not need residences. My life has been one long journey." He spent one out of every four days of his reign on the road, from Antwerp in Belgium to Seville in Spain, and Naples, Italy, to Frankfurt, Germany.

For a while it looked as if his son Philip II might do the same. But, after becoming ruler, Philip retreated more and more to Spain, choosing a capital at Madrid and building a huge, gloomy palace, the Escorial, in the countryside. There he gathered reports from the empire, relying on them for accuracy. The reports often conflicted, and then he had to ask for even more reports. No wonder he became known as the "paper king." One critic referred to him as "the black spider in his bleak cell at the Escorial."

1492, A REMARKABLE YEAR

In the early days of the Spanish Empire, however, everyone seemed in motion, not just the rulers. Much of that motion was involuntary, as Spain's determined Catholic leaders pushed out non-Catholics. The Spanish slave trade took millions of Africans to the Americas, and hundreds of thousands of impoverished Spaniards left Spain hoping to find wealth and

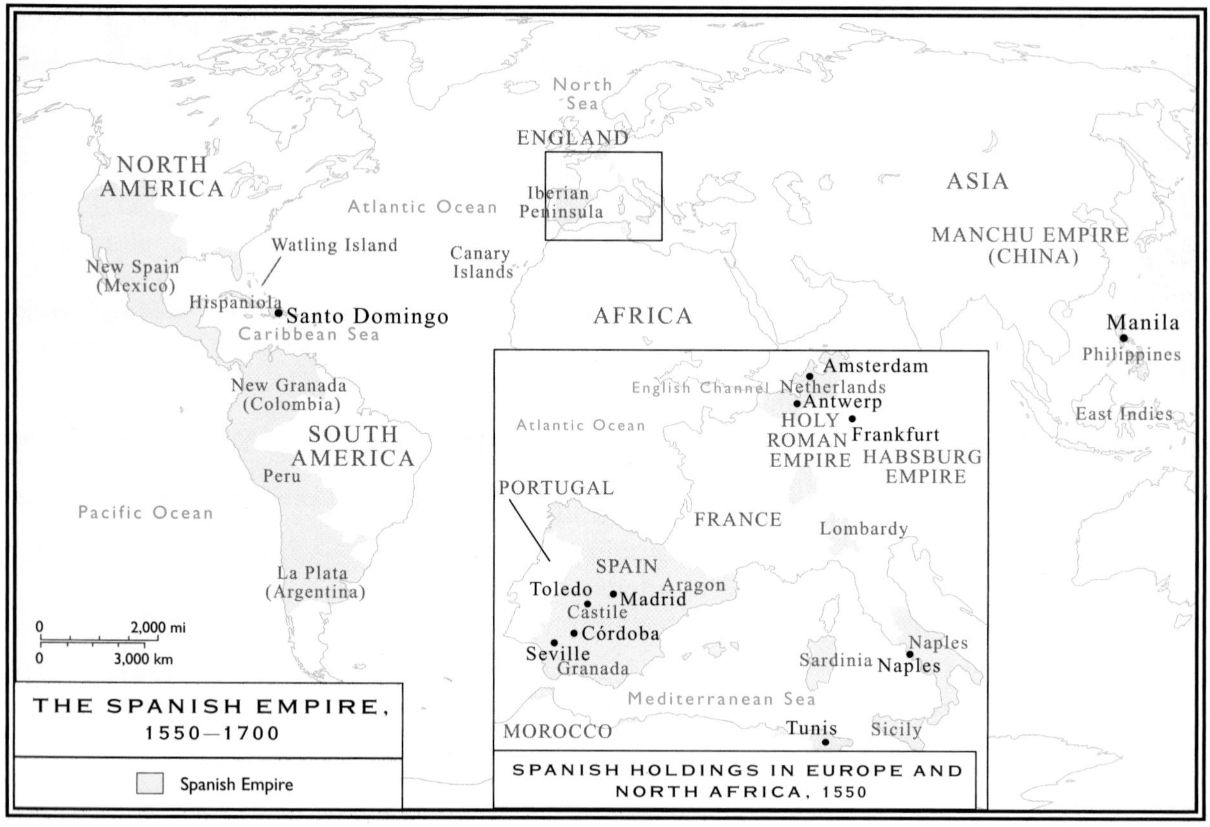

THE SPANISH EMPIRE, 1550–1700

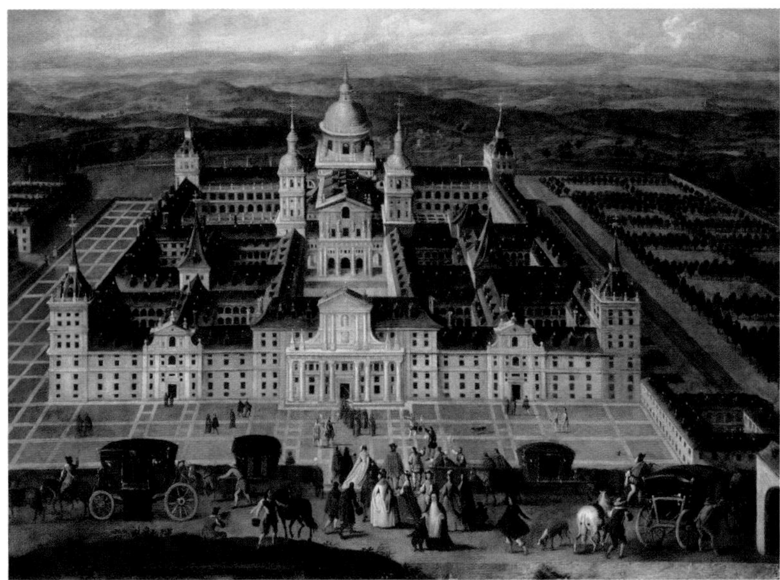

Philip II's Escorial Palace sits on an isolated plain where he could surround himself with his papers, his court, and art. "Your Majesty is a like a blind man who has excellent understanding, but can only see exterior objects through the eyes of those who describe them to you," wrote Catholic missionary Geronimo de Mendieta from the Americas in 1560.

better lives in Spain's new colonies. No wonder that the great Spanish literary achievement of this age was the novel *The History of Don Quixote de la Mancha* by Miguel de Cervantes, first published in 1603. Don Quixote, the hero, sets out to "make a knight errant of himself, roaming the world over in full armor and on horseback in quest of adventure."

There was more than enough adventure as three major events rocked the Spanish-speaking world in 1492. First, Ferdinand and Isabella took the city of Granada, the last major stronghold of Muslim power in Spain. Arabs had taken the Iberian Peninsula in 711 and, as the saying went, "What was lost in seven years took 700 to recover." The Arabs had brought much to Spain: fruit crops grown using irrigation, a thriving silk trade, contact with ancient philosophy and science through Arab translation of ancient texts, and Muslim architecture. Even the Spanish rulers recognized that the magnificent mosque in Córdoba, with 1,000 columns, and the palace of the Alhambra in Granada were masterpieces. Ferdinand and Isabella had the following inscription, a poem by the Spaniard Francisco de Icaza, placed at the entrance of the Alhambra where the poor might beg: "Give him alms, woman, for there is nothing in life, nothing so sad as to be blind in Granada."

In the courtyard of the Moorish palace of the Alhambra in Granada, lions guard a central fountain. Although the Alhambra symbolized Muslim culture and architecture, Spanish monarchs were so impressed that they could not bear to dismantle it.

For many, there was something sadder still: to lose Granada, their religion, and their lives. Ferdinand and, particularly, Isabella were fervent Roman Catholics and believed that Muslims had no place in their lands. An earlier king of Castile had promised Arabs that they might continue to practice their religion, speak Arabic, and wear their traditional clothing, including veils for women. In 1492, however, the monarchs gave the people of Granada the choice of conversion to Christianity or expulsion from Spain. At this time, about 60,000 Muslims went to North Africa, leaving behind their homes and goods to the triumphant Spanish knights. Most of the rest converted, becoming known as *moriscos;* Isabella promised these people the right to keep their language and dress.

The Inquisition, brought to Spain in 1478, was a court of inquiry to make sure newly converted subjects and other Catholics followed official Catholic doctrine. One of the most suspicious actions a *morisco* could take—ironically, considering the poor hygiene at the time—was to bathe. Because Muslims are required to be clean before prayers, frequent washing seemed to be an indication of heresy, or belief in a religion other than Catholicism. After a *morisco* revolt in 1570, Spanish officials ordered that the *moriscos* be moved from Granada and scattered all over Spain. Don Juan of Austria, a Spanish commander and the illegitimate son of Charles V, was moved by their plight: "It was the saddest sight in the world for at the time they set out there was so much rain, wind and snow that mothers had to abandon their children by the wayside and wives their husbands." Between 1609 and 1611, all the *moriscos* were forced to leave Spain.

The second important event of 1492 was Ferdinand's and Isabella's decision to expel from Spain Jews who refused to convert to Christianity. Jews had been in Spain for centuries and had made major contributions in medicine and philosophy. The Jews of Toledo, in particular, had translated from Arabic many of the Greek and Roman texts that later formed the basis of Renaissance thought. Using bribery, one of the Jewish leaders, Abrahanel, almost convinced Ferdinand to revoke the expulsion decree. But the leader of the Inquisition, Torquemada, cautioned Ferdinand that if he revoked the decree it would be like Judas taking silver from the Romans to betray Jesus.

Jews faced poor conditions whether they left Spain or converted to Christianity and stayed. If they went, they had to leave behind any wealth they had and then rebuild their lives in a strange land. If they stayed in Spain and converted to Catholicism, they were labeled *conversos,* or converted ones, and Inquisition spies checked to see if they still followed any Jewish practices, such as not eating pork. *Conversos* became some of the most noted Catholic religious figures of the time. Isabella's own priest, Talavera, had a Jewish background. Teresa of Avila, founder of the Carmelite Order of nuns and a mystic religious writer, had a *converso* grandfather who was brought before the Inquisition. Her seven brothers all went to Peru "to get themselves far away from

"Potosi lives in order to serve the imposing aspirations [hopes] of Spain: it serves to chastise [defeat] the Turk, humble the Moor, make Flanders tremble and terrify England."

—A Spanish friar describing Potosi, a silver mine in central Peru, 1630

Spain in order to escape painful gossip." Gossip, neighbors settling scores, or political rivalries often formed the basis of Inquisition investigations. *Conversos* were never quite safe.

The third major event in 1492 was, of course, Christopher Columbus's voyage to explore the western Atlantic. Isabella was the main sponsor of the voyage; she was, after all, the great-niece of Henry the Navigator of Portugal. Ferdinand, on the other hand, was primarily concerned with leading Spanish armies, which he did well. Columbus first brought his plan to reach the Spice Islands of Asia by sailing west to the Portuguese. The king was intrigued by Columbus's idea, but sent it to a naval committee. They had a much better sense than Columbus of how vast the distance was to China and believed a crew would run out of water and food before landfall.

Columbus was wrong in his sense of distance, but right in believing, based on his observations of birds and seeds washing ashore in the Canary Islands off the coast of North Africa, that land was relatively close—somewhere. Though others had tried sailing west and were lost, Columbus's great advantage was his understanding of the trade winds near the Canary Islands. Instead of sailing directly west, he would first go south, and then turn and catch the winds that would push his ships west. Columbus tried to get Spanish support and was turned down at first. Ferdinand and Isabella had spent heavily to defeat the Arabs. Should he try France? Isabella, who had already pawned her jewels for the Granada campaign, stepped in and convinced some rich Spaniards to lend her the money for the voyage.

St. Dominic directs Inquisition officials as they prepare to burn heretics, those who were judged to have violated Catholic religious doctrine. In addition to the thousands killed in the Inquisition, many Jews, Arabs, and Protestants fled Spain during this period, taking their talents for trade, agriculture, and science with them.

With his three ships, the *Nina,* the *Pinta,* and the *Santa Maria,* Columbus left Spain on August 3, 1492, and landed on Watling Island in the Caribbean on October 12, 1492. Throughout three more voyages, Columbus believed that he had reached the East Indies, even carrying with him a letter to the great khan. Evidence—no Chinese court, no spices, another ocean—gradually convinced Europeans that two whole continents existed between themselves and Asia. Peoples on both sides of the Atlantic adjusted their thinking about a new diversity of foods, animals, and customs. Spanish adventurers pushed into the interior of North and South America with hundreds of explorations. Fighting disease, jungle conditions, and terrible storms, Bernal Diaz de Castillo probably spoke for most of the voyagers about why they did it: "We came here to serve God and the king, and also to get rich." Where was the wealth? The explorer Hernán Cortés found it in the ancient American civilizations of Mexico, and another explorer, Francisco Pizarro, in Peru. Vasco de Balboa found emeralds in Colombia and a new ocean, the Pacific, on the other side of the Americas.

"The men became so weak that the poor women had to do all their work; they had to wash their clothes and care of them when sick, to cook the little food they had; stand sentinel, care for the watchfire and prepare the crossbows when the Indians attacked and even fire the petronels [firearms]."

—Isabel de Guevara, letter to Princess Dona Juana of Spain describing the settlement at River Rio de La Plata, Argentina, 1556

The costs of all this exploration were heavy, and the people of the Americas bore much of the burden. Initial contact between American Indians and Europeans was often friendly. In 1493, Columbus found the Caribbean Taino Indians to be "affectionate and without covetousness.... They love their neighbor as themselves." Cortés, Balboa, and Pizarro also met people curious about the European visitors and willing to show them their lands. But then tensions would start over women and goods. Spanish men, for the most part, came without women and began to capture and rape native women. Searching for gold, some Spaniards allowed their crews to torture Indians to see if they knew where the mines were.

As the Spanish gradually defeated the peoples who fought them, a debate arose among Spanish officials about how to rule the Americas. Isabella viewed Indians as her "vassals," or subjects, who, once converted to Christianity, would go about their lives as Spaniards did. The conquistadors, leaders in the conquest of the New World, saw the inhabitants of America as part of an *encomienda* system of plantationlike farms on which they, as the large landowners, would use the people of America as servants. Columbus

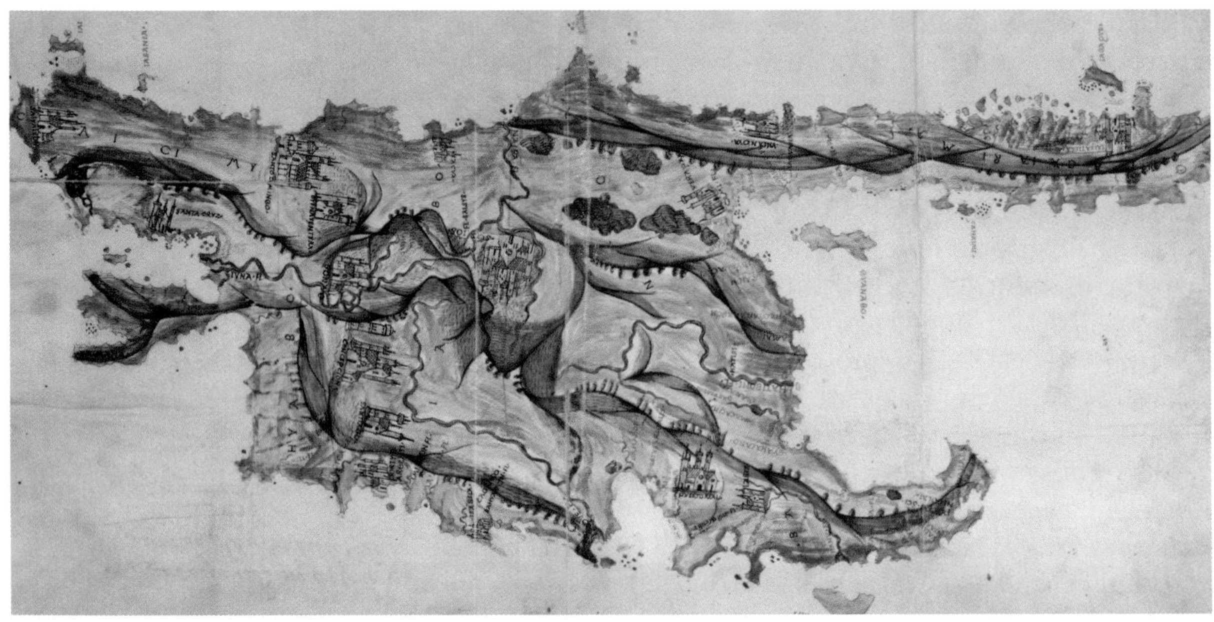

On a 16th-century map of Santo Domingo, where Columbus landed in 1493, the island seems lush with plants and open to settlement. Establishing permanent outposts, however, did not prove easy; of the 1,200 colonists who came in 1493, barely 200 remained 25 years later.

praised life in Hispaniola (now the Dominican Republic and Haiti) in 1498: "Of our people here, each has two or three Indians to serve him."

Above all, however, the monarchs were disturbed by reports about how brutally Spaniards treated Indians in the fields, mines, and weaving factories. Men such as the missionary Bartolomé de Las Casas, grandson of a *converso* burned by the Inquisition, spoke out against the Spanish landlords for "their blindness, their injustices, their tyrannies and their cruelties." The Catholic Church proposed a mission system. Native Americans would be gathered near a church with a military outpost nearby. Here priests would teach Indians to be good Catholics and dress as Europeans. The Indians would also provide the labor that supported the missions.

A devastating but unanticipated outcome of bringing Native Americans into close contact with Europeans was the spread of disease. Smallpox, measles, mumps, yellow fever, and other diseases were unknown in the Americas before Europeans arrived. In the valley of Mexico alone there were 50 epidemics from 1519 to 1810. A Mexica woman in the 17th century remembered a time when children were plentiful. Now, she told a translator, "Hardly anyone who is born grows up, they just all die off." Another sad outcome of these epidemics, devastating the Indian population, was that African slaves were brought to the Americas to replace their labor. Critics of enslaving Native Americans, such as Las Casas, did not protest. Las Casas actually encouraged such importation because he thought it was a way of saving Indians. Some priests did criticize African slavery, as Jesuit Alonso de Sandoval did in 1627. He wrote to the Spanish government that slavery "is a perpetual death, a living death in which people die even while they are alive."

Despite the spread of disease and violence against them, Native Americans resisted the Spanish. In the southwest of what would become the United States, Pueblo Indians made war against the Spanish in 1680. The Pueblo, particularly, objected to Franciscan missionaries interfering with their mask dances and then whipping 47 of their elders in public. Their war leaders organized nearly 17,000 Hopi and others to fight the Spanish. It took almost 20 years for the Spanish to regain control.

"The distress of my son who was with me racked my soul, for he was only thirteen years old, and he was not only exhausted but remained so for a very long time. But the Lord gave him such courage that he cheered the others, and he worked as hard on the ship as if he had been a sailor for eighty years. He comforted me, for I, too had fallen ill."

—Christopher Columbus, *Recollections of Christopher Columbus on his Fourth and Last Voyage*, 1502

ENEMIES AT EVERY TURN

All these American events were described by Spanish officials in piles upon piles of requests, reports, debates, and Inquisition records. No wonder that Philip II, squeezing in an appointment, protested, "Just look at the back-log of papers I shall have!" No wonder that he, like Philip III and Philip IV, turned to art as an escape. Their support of artists such as Diego Velazquez, El Greco, Bartolomé Murillo, Sofonisba Anguissola, Francisco de Zurbarán, and Jusepe Ribera helped to create the Golden Age of Spanish painting. During this period Spanish artists added dramatic lighting and realism to their canvases even as the Inquisition drew up more lists of rules in an attempt to force artists to focus on religious subjects.

The empire of Spain included not only the Americas, but also a good part of Europe, with enemies in all directions. To the west was Portugal, Spain's rival for the Canary

A Priest Speaks Out

REGINALDO DE MONTESINOS, SERMON DELIVERED IN A DOMINICAN CHURCH, 1511

Reginaldo de Montesinos, a Dominican missionary to Santo Domingo, gave a strong sermon there on December 4, 1511. In the audience were Diego Colón, Columbus's son, and other officials and prominent settlers who were stunned by his harshness in defending the Native Americans.

This voice [divine judgment] says that you are in moral sin, that you are living and may die in it, because of the cruelty and tyranny which you use in dealing with these innocent people. Tell me, by what right or by what interpretation of justice do you keep these Indians in such a cruel and horrible servitude? By what authority have you waged such detestable wars against people who were once living quietly and peacefully in their own lands? . . . Why do you keep those who survive so oppressed and weary, not giving them enough to eat, not caring for them in their illnesses? For, with the excessive work you demand of them, they fall ill and die or, rather, you kill them with your desire to extract and acquire more gold every day. And what care do you take that they be instructed in religion, that they know God, the creator, and that they are baptized and hear Mass, keeping Holy days and Sundays? . . . Are these not men? Have they no rational souls? Are you not bound to love them as you love yourselves?

Armored Spanish soldiers tortured and killed thousands of Native Americans during their 1588 conquest of Mexico. Not only were Native Americans mistreated physically, but their cultural heritage suffered as well: missionaries burned many Aztec and Maya books.

The painter Diego Velazquez portrayed ordinary life in his work entitled Old Woman Cooking Eggs. *According to the Inquisition, the proper subject of painting in 17th-century Spain was religion—even dogs and cats had to be removed from religious art. As Philip II's favorite painter and the son-in-law of an art censor, Velazquez could get away with more than many of his contemporaries could.*

Islands, the spice trade, South America, and control of the Iberian Peninsula, where Spain and Portugal are both located. With the Portuguese, Philip II got lucky; his mother had been a Portuguese princess, and he inherited the Portuguese throne. To the south, Spanish rulers continued their crusade against Muslims with invasions of Morocco and Tunis, a city in Tunisia. To the east lay Italy, where the Spanish controlled the states of Naples, Sicily, Sardinia, and other parts of the peninsula. France tried to gain control of northern Italy in 1515 but was beaten back by Spain's forces after 16 years of fighting.

To the north, there were two main enemies: Holland and England. Of them, the Dutch may have damaged the Spanish most, even though Holland was a small nation. They were, as the English traveler Owen Feltham wrote in 1652, "the little sword-fish pricking the bellies of the whale." The Spanish Netherlands, in the 16th century, included today's Holland, Belgium, and Luxembourg, with 17 provinces in all. The Dutch-speaking provinces became largely Protestant during the 16th-century revolt against the Catholic Church known as the Reformation, and were led by the tough ruler William of Orange. Spanish officials

The chains of former slaves hang on the monastery walls of Castilla La Mancha in Toledo, Spain. Christians forced into slavery by the Moors and freed by Isabella and Ferdinand donated their chains to the church in gratitude.

thought that by ridding themselves of him, they could stop the rebellion taking place in the Netherlands. As one Spanish soldier said, "All the time I was in Flanders, I did nothing except try to find someone who would kill the prince of Orange." Philip's agents finally managed to assassinate William in 1584.

Philip was determined to prevent Protestant "heretics," or non-Catholics, from taking over an area so valuable to Spain. Spain's wool went to looms in the Netherlands to be processed, and the bankers of Antwerp and Amsterdam provided the efficient banking system that was missing in Spain. The Spanish conducted a brutal war against the Netherlands, massacring 2,300 troops after the Dutch defeat at Haarlem (a city in Holland), and sacking the city of Antwerp. This costly war ended only after Philip's death, when the Netherlands was allowed to become independent.

Philip was also obsessed with conquering England, another "heretic" nation in his eyes. Philip's plan was to build a huge fleet of ships, the Grand Armada, to sail up from Spain, collect Spanish troops in the Netherlands, and ferry them across the English Channel to England. Philip's generals thought the plan was risky. The English Navy was skilled, and bad weather made crossing the channel unpredictable. Philip's answer to these challenges was, "We are fully aware of the risk... but since it is all for His cause, God will send good weather."

The English defeated the Spanish Armada in 1588. The English sent boats that were on fire into the middle of the Spanish fleet and then moved in to hit the scattered ships with their long-range guns. As the English chased the Spanish into the North Sea, a storm sank even more Spanish ships.

As Spain squandered the wealth it received from the Americas on foreign military adventures, it neglected to develop its own resources. It ignored new technologies and did not spend money on education. The port of Seville was allowed to fill with mud, so ships could no longer reach it. A canal from Toledo, linking the Tagus River to the sea to form a silk route, was started in 1587, but then dropped. As the Duke of Sesse during Philip's reign put it, "We flit so rapidly from one area to another, without making a major effort in one and then, when that is finished, in another. . . . I do not know why we eat so many snacks but never a real meal!" By the 1700s, Spain still had much of its American empire, but there new societies were developing with their own values and power. In Europe, Spain's prestige declined as well. The poet and soldier Garcilaso de la Vega wrote in 1535, perhaps anticipating later difficulties: "And everything is gone, even the name of house and home and wife and memory. And what's the use of it? A little fame? The nation's thanks? A place in history? One day they'll write a book and then we'll see."

"He [Ferdinand] has continually contrived great things, which have kept his subjects' minds uncertain and astonished and occupied in watching their result. And these actions have arisen one out of the other, so that they have left no time for men to settle down and act against him."

—Niccolò Machiavelli, *The Prince*, 1513

The large-sterned ships of the Spanish Armada line up in a crescent formation as smaller English vessels prepare to attack them in the English Channel. The Spanish were expecting ship-to-ship fighting, in which their higher decks would be an advantage, but the English relied on long-range guns and quick maneuvers to win the naval battle.

CHAPTER 10

THE WEDDING RING EMPIRE

EUROPE UNDER THE HABSBURGS

The Habsburg Empire, with its capital in Vienna, was a work in progress that lasted for nearly 500 years. Unlike other empires built by the energy of an individual or the force of an idea, a complex set of central European marriages created its territory. As the saying went, "Let the strong fight wars. You, happy Austria, marry!" Known as the Wedding Ring Empire, the House of the Habsburg, or the Austrian Empire, it controlled different areas at different times, rather like a house that was continually being remodeled. After the sudden death of a Hungarian or Spanish king, there was bound to be a Habsburg relative to claim his throne. From 1643 to 1679, for example, the Spanish Habsburgs married 14 times within their branch and 6 times with the German branch of the family.

Sitting beneath his royal coat of arms, Charles V can also be identified as a Habsburg emperor by the characteristic family trait: a prominent jaw. Tired of trying to control a vast empire almost constantly at war, he wrote "I wish for peace, I wish for peace, I wish for peace," when Francis I of France invaded Habsburg Italy.

The downside of all these marriages among relatives was some disabling physical traits, mental retardation, and the jutting "Habsburg jaw" that made even drinking water difficult for some family members. Some of them were so focused on family tradition that they were not open to new ideas. The upside was that the Habsburgs were like a family business, using their princes and princesses, archdukes and duchesses to care for the empire. For example, four of the Habsburg grand duchesses tended the Netherlands at its height. One of these, Margaret of Parma, was also a diplomat, negotiating with the French duchess Louise of Savoy to cement a "Ladies' Peace" in 1520 between France and the Habsburgs. The emperor was rather like a stage director, handing out parts to the Habsburg Players.

OUT OF MANY, ONE

The name Habsburg comes from the title of the family's military castle, built around 1020—Habichtsburg, or Hawk's castle. The family's holdings were in Switzerland, but over the years they lost that territory. By 1500 or so, they controlled the area that is now Austria, parts of northern Italy, Germany around the Rhineland, Belgium, the Czech Republic, Slovakia, Hungary, and other areas of the Balkans. When their holdings became so vast, the family split. While the Spanish Habsburgs saw Spain, Portugal, southern Italy, and the Americas as their sphere of influence, the German Habsburgs aimed at controlling central Europe. One of the ways to do so was to become head of the Holy Roman Empire, a collection of about 350 mainly German-speaking states. Almost always, the head of the German Habsburg family was elected emperor.

THE HABSBURG EMPIRE, 1700s

"Although I am very industrious, I am the harshest hater of work. But I work for my thirst of knowledge. I am never lacking an object of my desire, my burning eagerness, to do research on difficult matters."

—Scientist Johannes Kepler, "Self-Characterization," 1597

All these marriages meant serious complications for the people of these areas, who had their own languages and customs, and who often resented the German-speaking Habsburgs. Each area also had its own enemies—Burgundy had France; and the Ottomans threatened Bohemia and Hungary. From 1500 to 1750, the Habsburgs had three main problems: dealing with the Reformation, defeating the Ottomans, and ensuring a peaceful succession of power. The Habsburgs did maintain their empire as primarily Catholic, their armies did force the Ottomans back, and their dynasty lasted until 1918. But their successes came at a high price.

The German Habsburgs, like their relative Philip II of Spain, were staunch Catholics who believed it was their duty to stamp out heresy. In Bohemia, Jan Hus challenged the Catholic Church. Hus was a Czech clergyman who wanted a reformed church, including a Bible translated so people could read it in their own language. He also sought to limit the wealth of the church, and to end the selling of church positions. At the Council of Constance, where he was called and told he would be protected, Hus presumed to lecture the emperor Sigismund on the purity of his own religion, to which the emperor replied, "none of us is without sin, Jan Hus."

The promise to protect Hus was taken back on the grounds that it was not necessary to keep faith with heretics, and in 1415, Hus was condemned and burned at the stake. His death did not end the reform movement, and a century later, Martin Luther, a northern German, challenged the church with his "Ninety-Five Theses," or ways to change religious doctrine. The Habsburgs, though fighting to preserve Catholicism, came to accept a treaty in 1555 known as the Peace of Augsburg that established the principle *cuius regio, eius religio*: the religion of the ruler would determine the religion of the subjects. For half a century, the Habsburg rulers were relatively tolerant.

Ferdinand II had been raised in Spain as a strict Catholic and returned to Germany determined to halt the growing Protestant movement there. Unlike earlier Habsburg rulers,

Jan Hus, a Czech church reformer, sits atop a woodpile, waiting to be burned as a heretic. The witnesses are Inquisition judges and Habsburg officials. Hus wanted a Czech translation of the Latin Bible that would allow ordinary people to read the holy book.

Ferdinand II believed that all his subjects had to share his Catholic beliefs and put pressure on Protestants to convert. The experiences of the scientist Johannes Kepler give some idea of the kinds of methods Ferdinand and other Habsburgs used to harass non-Catholics.

Johannes Kepler was the scientist and mathematician who met Danish astronomer Tycho Brahe in Prague and used Brahe's measurements of the position of the planets to modify Copernicus's view of the solar system. Kepler was puzzled by the orbit of planets, which sped up as they approached the sun. Through much hard work, Kepler figured out that planets do not move in perfect circles around the sun, but in elliptical paths. He also developed sets of tables to determine when and where planets would be at different times of the year. But as a Protestant under

Ferdinand II, he faced discrimination. He lost his teaching job, had to leave his town, and even had trouble finding a gravesite for his daughter. His mother was accused of witchcraft and imprisoned. Only his reputation as a scientist kept her from being hanged. Yet, as he packed to leave his town, he wrote a friend, "I would not have thought that it is so sweet in companionship with some brothers, to suffer injustice and indignity for the sake of religion, to abandon house, family, friends and homeland."

These religious differences led to one of the most devastating wars in European history, the Thirty Years' War, from 1618 to 1648 when Catholic Habsburgs fought Protestant German states and their allies. As armies moved throughout the countryside, they brought plague and smallpox, destroyed crops, and created famines. In some areas, 40 percent of the villages were destroyed; Pomerania,

Bohemian (Czech) Protestants throw Catholic Habsburg governors out of the window of Prague Castle in 1618, an event called the Defenestration of Prague. The governors survived, landing on a soft manure pile below, but the incident caused the Habsburg emperor Ferdinand II to brutally retaliate.

in northern Germany, saw a 65 percent drop in population. Looters ransacked churches. A Catholic officer was dismayed that attackers "left not a single stall intact; altars were knocked down, images broken and missals torn up . . . [by] men who are not soldiers but assassins."

The Thirty Years' War began after two incidents of religious intolerance. In Prague, after authorities turned down a request to build more Protestant churches, the Czechs rebelled and the nearby state of Saxony, part of present-day Germany, joined them in fighting the Habsburg Army. Basically untrained, the Czech forces were defeated at the Battle of White Mountain in 1620. The second incident occurred when the Habsburgs moved into the Protestant independent city of Donaworth in western Germany. Since Ferdinand, as Holy Roman Emperor, was supposed to protect the liberties of Germany, this attack on a member city brought several German states into the war. Later the German states would be joined by Denmark, the Netherlands, and Sweden, all united against the Habsburgs.

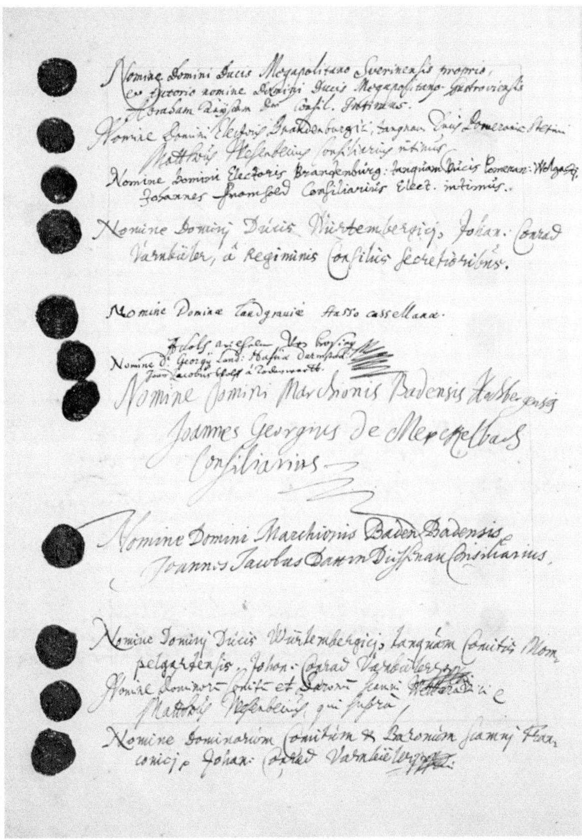

A page from the Treaty of Westphalia signed in 1648 would have been a welcome sight to participants of the Thirty Years' War, which tore apart central Europe. Although it did not guarantee individual religious freedom, it did permit Catholic, Lutheran, and Calvinist rulers to set up their own state religions.

At first, the Habsburg Army did very well, particularly under the direction of General Albrecht von Wallenstein, who had about 130,000 mercenary troops fighting with him. But the Swedes were a determined enemy, and their warrior king, Gustavus Adolphus, could match Wallenstein in military strategy. After a series of victories, Adolphus was killed while leading his troops at the Battle of Lutzen. Strangely, perhaps influenced by his Protestant relatives, General Wallenstein did not vigorously pursue the Swedish Army. Sensing a conspiracy against him, Ferdinand had Wallenstein arrested and assassinated. The soldiers sang about Wallenstein: "For that's what happens when one is too ambitious / The Devil silently comes / And trips him up." The Treaty of Westphalia in 1648 ended the war, confirming the idea that a monarch could determine the religion of the lands he ruled.

Fortunately for the Habsburgs, the Ottomans had been relatively quiet during the years when fighting was centered in northern Europe. But in 1683, the Ottomans tried again to take Vienna. When the Ottoman Army approached the city, Emperor Leopold I left Vienna and took refuge 175 miles away in Passau, now part of Germany. The Polish king Jan Sobieski stepped in and beat back the Ottomans. In spite of the flight of their emperor, the Viennese could be proud of their mayor and the 600 University of Vienna students who stayed to defend the city. Croissants, rolls baked to make fun of the Turkish flag with its the crescent insignia, originate from those days.

One of the brave young soldiers at the siege of Vienna was Eugene of Savoy. Like Wallenstein, he became one of

With the towers of Prague in the distance, the armies of the Czechs and Saxons meet Habsburg forces at the Battle of White Mountain in 1620. Although the Habsburgs maintained control of their economically valuable province by defeating the hastily gathered alliance, the battle became a symbol of Czech resistance.

the Habsburg's greatest generals. Eugene had a rather mysterious past. His father, though Italian, fought with the French Army, and his mother was the niece of the cardinal Mazarin, a powerful French church leader. Eugene's mother was known for her affairs, and it is fairly likely one was with the French king Louis XIV. For some reason, Louis banished Eugene's mother and refused to let Eugene follow his father into the French military. Eugene then went to the Habsburgs and took revenge by beating Louis's armies. After one raid on French soil, Eugene said to a friend, "Didn't I say I would only return to France, sword in hand?"

> *"Hasten, use your common sense,*
> *Before the whole of Europe goes up in smoke,*
> *Believe me, avoiding wars is more*
> *Than a thousand victories."*
>
> —Silesian poet Andreas Scultetus, 17th century

With Eugene of Savoy at the head of their army, the Habsburgs, with the aid of Hungarian, Serbian, Polish, and Croatian fighters, pushed the Ottomans back from central Europe. The Habsburgs also called on Eugene's services in other wars that involved new rulers replacing old ones in Spain, Poland, and Austria. These wars, which lasted for about a dozen years, raise the issue of whether the Habsburgs used the resources of their lands wisely, or whether they were simply out to add more crowns to their empire, regardless of any economic gain. Eugene of Savoy despaired of getting the three emperors he served to take a long view of Habsburg interests. Leopold I kept writing him letters to "act cautiously," even when the Austrians were under attack. The problems of Europe, Eugene wrote sarcastically to a friend, "certainly disturbed the Emperor [Leopold] for the space of an hour. But luckily on the same day, there was a procession, and he forgot anything else."

Unfortunately, others also felt remote from the Habsburg center of power. The Hungarians, finally freed from the Turks, tried to reclaim their earlier independence. Aided by the *kuruc*, Hungarian guerrilla fighters, the Hungarians revolted. This led to the harsh conditions described by a son of James II of England in 1686. "Hungary" he wrote, "is the miserablest country in the world, for it is plundered every day or else by the Christians or the Turks or sometimes by both."

The Hungarians were only one of 10 major language groups the Habsburg had to recognize, and many of them began to resent the German-speaking officials collecting

Known for his extensive war preparations, Habsburg general Eugene of Savoy sits astride his charger ready to do battle. The duke of Marbourgh, amazed by the general's successes, wrote of him, "Why did the Prince consider so many possibilities when one was enough for victory?"

their taxes and running their government offices. In the early 18th century, under Charles VI, the empire was adrift, nearly bankrupt from war, and in comparison to the rising powers of Prussia and Russia, much less feared by its neighbors. The only real issue Charles seemed concerned about was his successor, as he had no sons or living brothers who would rule after him. Desperate to keep the throne in the family, Charles proposed in 1713 a suspension of the laws, called the Pragmatic Sanction, which would allow his daughter Maria Theresa to be monarch. He promised bribes to various nations if they would agree. After eating a plate of bad mushrooms, Charles died in 1740, before he was able to take care of the details of his daughter's accession to the throne and the bribes for loyalty to Maria Theresa went unpaid. It was, the French writer Voltaire said, "the pot of mushrooms which changed the course of history." His death certainly changed Maria Theresa's life.

THE QUEEN OF COMMON SENSE

Considering how much energy Charles had put into the Pragmatic Sanction, it is odd that he did not think of preparing his daughter to take the throne. Outside of the usual religious processions, Maria Theresa had mainly appeared in public as a singer, sometimes accompanied at the harpsichord by her father. As Maria Theresa wrote, "It never pleased my father's Majesty to have me present when he transacted business, domestic or foreign."

Her Majesty's Busy Schedule

EMANUEL TAROUCA, LETTER TO EMPRESS MARIA THERESA, 1740

Because Maria Theresa had little practice in statecraft when she came to the Habsburg throne in 1740, she asked a trusted adviser and soldier, Portuguese count Emanuel Tarouca, to observe her activities. Tarouca's proposed schedule, outlined in a letter, gives an insight into her busy times and shows which parts of her schedule she valued. Besides being ruler, Maria Theresa eventually had 16 children with her husband, the duke of Lorraine, whom she adored.

I [Tarouca] assume Your Majesty will rise shortly after eight o'clock. You will be occupied till nine with your prayers, attending Mass . . . while the coffee is getting cold! Spoiled coffee may upset the stomach.

Knowing how little time is devoted to Your Majesty's [getting dressed], I put down only half an hour for it. After which, as a good mother, you should inquire about the royal family.

From 9:30 to 11 Your Majesty should use the time in reading, or listening to, the reports of the ministers, granting one audience a week to some of them, two to some others. . . . My suggestion aims at keeping the minister from importuning Your Majesty, as well as saving them time. Also, their reports will be shorter that way. . . .

Now I come back to the morning hours. At 11:30 the private secretary must be ready in the antechamber to be handed the papers disposed of and the orders written out. . . . I assume Your Majesty will sit down at table at 12:15 and rise at 1:15. [From 1:30 to 3:30] Your Majesty should discharge family duties, giving them as much of your time as body and soul require on a particular day; human nature refused to be the same all the time.

At 3:30 Your Majesty should return to the reports of the minister. . . . Then, until 6, you might receive some of the chamberlains of Privy Councilors. At 6 o'clock, with the secretary dismissed, you still have two and a half hours until supper time, my opinion being that Your Majesty under all circumstances must have supper at 8:30. The first half of those two and a half hours will be for Vespers or the Rosary, the second for listening to someone who has been asked, and also for praying or amusing yourself.

She had a rocky beginning. As she put it, "I do not think anyone would deny that history hardly knows of a crowned head who started his rule under circumstances more grievous than those attending my accession." Frederick the Great of Prussia had sent her a letter of his "most deepest sympathy" at her father's death. But in 1740 he quickly invaded the Habsburg province of Silesia and added it to his kingdom. Maria Theresa's distant relative King Charles of Bavaria joined with Frederick in an attempt to dethrone her. A woman of great common sense, Maria Theresa realized that she had to assert herself to be seen the legitimate ruler of the Habsburgs.

Empress Maria Theresa travels in her carriage to the front lines to encourage her Habsburg troops as they engage the Prussians in the War of Austrian Succession. It was especially important for her to be visible to her army because the war was largely fought over whether a woman had a right to rule the empire.

> *"You, the heads of Christiandom, cannot reap at home the honor you have lost by failing to pursue the Turks."*
>
> —Margaret of Parma, grand duchess of the Habsburgs and regent in the Netherlands, in a letter criticizing her nephews Charles V and Ferdinand I's priorities in European wars, 1520s

She began to build forces against Frederick. Though her father's advisers urged caution, Maria Theresa wrote to one: "You had better realize that no one is to be trusted less than the Prussians." One of the first places she went for help was to the Diet, the political assembly, of Hungary. She wore a Hungarian dress, requested the Hungarians' assistance, and promised them more independent rights. Following her appearance in Hungary, the Habsburgs under Maria Theresa fought the Prussians to a standoff in a war that lasted eight years.

Prussia's rising power meant, at least in Maria Theresa's eyes, that reform could no longer be postponed. She started a military academy and created a more professional army. She tried to do something for the peasants, who were so burdened with taxes, church payments, and labor for nobles that they only kept three-fifths of what they earned. "The peasantry," she said, "must be able to sustain itself." When she discovered that half of her new advisers who supported the reforms had been educated in Protestant universities in northern Germany because subjects such as economics and political science were more advanced there, she upgraded the schools and universities in her empire.

With her diplomats, she started a reversal of alliances. The Habsburgs would put aside old French antagonisms and rely on France as an ally against Prussia. As a sign of this new reversal, Maria Theresa arranged the marriage of her daughter Marie Antoinette to Louis XVI of France. She had no way of knowing that she was dooming her daughter to the guillotine in the French Revolution.

By 1750, Maria Theresa and other Habsburgs recognized that mere protection of their family, their class—the

Habsburg royalty frequently visited the Marieselle Basilica in Austria, which was finished in the 17th century. Christian pilgrims would travel great distances to make offerings to the statue of Mary mounted on the church altar.

nobility—and their church was not enough for a modern nation. The interests of all her subjects had to be taken into account too. Though she remained prejudiced against Jews and Protestants, she promised, if not toleration for them, then at least freedom from persecution. But if the empire was no longer primarily the "House of Habsburg," what was it? In an empire in which no one called himself a "Habsburgian," but rather a Czech, Hungarian, Austrian, or even a Viennese, how could loyalty be continued when more rights were given? Issues surrounding nationality would later tear the Habsburg Empire apart as groups tried to claim their independence.

CHAPTER 11

TEENAGERS TAKE THE THRONE

MANCHU CHINA

Some of the best rulers in history started young. Two 13-year-old boys were the first Qing dynasty rulers of China. Not only were Shunzhi and Kangxi young, they were not even Chinese, but Manchus, a separate group of people from northeastern China. Their job in ruling China looked difficult. The previous dynasty, the Ming, had left them with major problems: taxes not collected, unread reports from neglectful Ming emperors, and inept officials

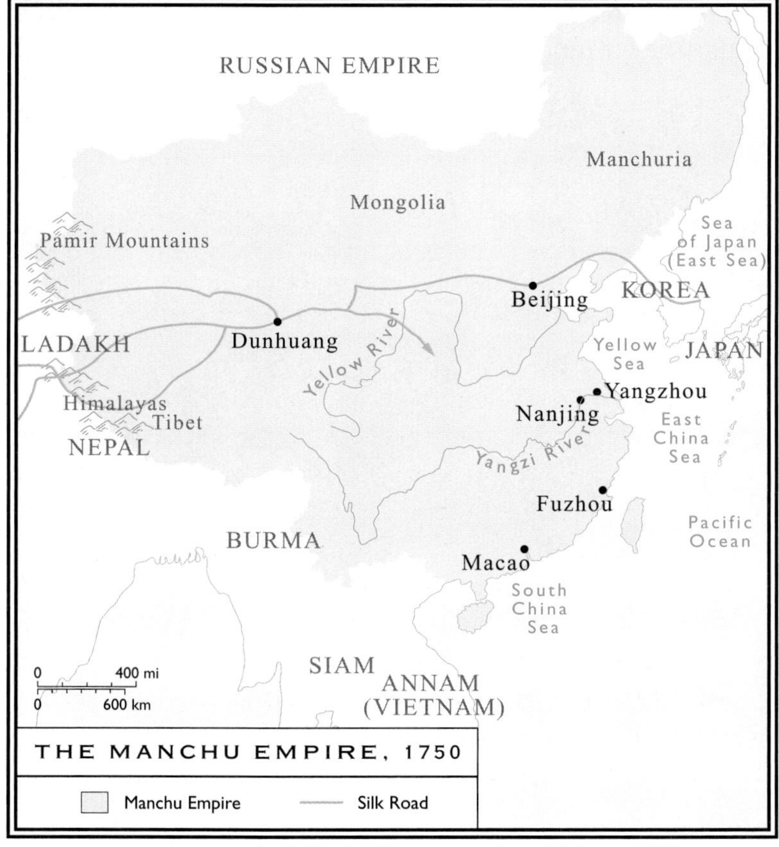

in the palace administration. In 1644, the last Ming emperor, Chongzhen, decided to commit suicide and ordered his wives and concubines to do the same. A note on his hanged body read: "I, feeble and of small virtue, have offended against Heaven, the rebels have seized my capital.... Ashamed to face my ancestors, I die."

The odds did not look good for the Manchus, with their population of 2 million people, to control China with its 100 million, even though they had a well-organized army and knowledge of Chinese administration. To add to the Manchus' trouble, their leader Abahai had been killed in earlier fighting. This is when five-year-old Shunzhi began his rule. When Shunzhi died in his 20s, his seven-year-old son Kangxi inherited the throne. Remarkably, Kangxi became one of the best Chinese emperors at a high point of Chinese history.

The Manchus made two major decisions about ruling China: they would keep their own Manchu language and

Accompanied by a mounted guard (right), Manchu emperor Kangxi, under a canopy, inspects a province in southern China. He saw all of China as his empire, yet favored northerners, writing, "The people of the North are strong, they must not copy the fancy diets of the Southerners who are physically frail."

Looking Out for the Little Guy

CHENG PANCH'IO, A LETTER TO HIS BROTHER, 1732

Cheng Panch'io was a Chinese poet, painter, and calligrapher who lived from 1693 to 1765. He was also a Qing magistrate and got into trouble with the governor of his province for trying to get more relief for the poor after a bad harvest. The letter quoted here, written in 1752 to his brother, shows his concern for the poor people whom the Qing were trying to bring into society more equally.

There is no one in the world who is not a descendant of the Yellow Emperor [the Chinese ancestor].... But today some have unfortunately become slaves, slave girls, concubines, and poor laborers, living in poverty and distress and unable to help themselves; it would be wrong to assume that their ancestors were slaves, slave girls, concubines, and poor laborers in generations ago. Once they make up their minds and are willing to work hard, some of them become rich and honored in their own life time; and others become so in the next generation. Some... taunt others on their birth and brag about their previous generations saying, "Who is he, and yet he is high up? I am such and such a person, and yet I am down and out. There is no justice in heaven or in the affairs of man." Also, they do not know that is exactly the justice of heaven and human affairs.... His ancestors were poor, and now it is his turn to be rich and honored; your ancestors were rich and honored and now it is your turn to be poor. Again, what is wrong with that?

After I... became a government graduate, whenever I found in the old trunks at our home some deed of a slave sold into our family in [a] former generation, I at once burned it over the oil lamp. I did not even return it to the person concerned, for I felt if I did it would be an obvious act and increase the man's embarrassment. Since I began to employ people, I have never required contracts. If we can get along with the servant, we keep him; and if not, we send him away. Why keep such a piece of paper to provide a pretext for our next generations to use it as a claim or a means of extortion? To act with such a heart is to have consideration for others, which is to have consideration for ourselves.

clan system and they would, within some limitations, respect Chinese culture. At times, they would collect Chinese art and literature to show how well they understood their subjects. But the Manchu had also seen the Yuan dynasty of the Mongols fall because rulers lost their Mongol customs and were overwhelmed by the Chinese. To prevent this, the Manchu closed Manchuria to Chinese settlement and planted a "willow wall" of trees in ditches several hundred miles long to limit how far north Chinese influence could go.

THE CIVILIZED BARBARIANS

Keeping their identity was difficult however, when they had to associate constantly with the more numerous Chinese, so Manchu leaders from the beginning made special arrangements for doing so. They made Chinese men shave the front of their heads and wear their hair in long queues, or ponytails. The Manchu said that made it easier to see who were friends and who were enemies in battle. The primary purpose probably was to show Manchu control.

The Manchu valued the image of the mounted warrior, and Manchu sons were raised to ride, shoot, and hunt. Kangxi, for example, had his sons practice archery and riding every day and delighted in such activities himself. As he wrote in a poem about one hunt,

> I'm going to stretch my limbs
> And keep on shooting the curved bow,
> Now with my left hand, now my right.

Twice a year, the Manchu went out from Beijing and joined their Mongol allies in major hunts. They enjoyed the informal camps and the excitement, and the long hours of riding as well as the killing of animals hardened men to wage wars. The Manchu could be as harsh as the Mongols had been to their enemies. When Ming forces held out against them at the Chinese city of Yangzhou, the Manchu warned the city to surrender or face terrible consequences. When the Manchu defeated the city, soldiers went on a 10-day rampage, killing

Because Manchu robes did not have pockets, men of the upper classes needed gilded brass belt attachments to carry their belongings. Everything from snuff bottles to scarves and swords were attached to these rings.

A Manchu nobleman and his servants prepare for a hunting excursion. Large hunts sponsored by the emperor were often the testing ground for tough, courageous behavior that would help to determine which of his sons might be chosen to rule.

as many people as they could. An anonymous account, later found in Japan, described how one man and his family lost their home, hid in huts near the cemetery, and then saw even those huts burned. As the author related, "The only recourse left was to go to the roadsides and lie among the corpses so that no one could tell us from the dead. My son, my wife, and I went and lay among the graves, so dirty and muddy from head to foot we did not look at all human."

The Manchu tried to maintain their language, religion, and class structure. Manchu officials developed a written language for the Manchu and schools in which this was taught. During the early Qing dynasty, top officials, whether Manchu or Chinese, were expected to use this language. When one Chinese official tried to use poor eyesight as an excuse for not writing in Manchu, Kangxi sharply asked him why his Chinese writing did not suffer equally.

Manchu families also kept their clan system and marriage customs. Their inheritance laws stated that a person's status as a noble would go up or down when a clan leader died. This acceptance of shifting fortunes may have been one of the reasons the Manchus discounted the Chinese Confucian system of "mean people." According to Confucian thought, certain groups, such as entertainers, leather workers, prostitutes, and gamblers, should not intermarry with others, nor should males from these groups be eligible to take Chinese examinations. The Manchu emperor, who believed in a less rigid class system, ruled in 1723 that these people should be treated like other Chinese.

The Manchu did believe in segregating themselves from Chinese society in a variety of ways. They did not marry Chinese, though they might marry an occasional Mongol woman, such as Kangxi's grandmother. They had seen how soon sons lost their Central Asian heritage if intermarriage took place; the Ottomans and Yuan dynasty proved that. Only the son of two Manchu parents could be emperor.

Embroidered flowers and bamboo leaves adorn a Manchu woman's colorful silk robe. A Manchu woman would probably also have worn a special butterfly hairstyle and platform shoes to make her feet look small, as if they were bound.

The Manchu also kept their customs concerning women and, at times, tried to extend them to the Chinese. The Manchu tried to outlaw the Chinese practice of foot binding. The feet of four- and five-year-old girls were tied together, heel to toe, with bandages to create a two-inch foot, which was considered attractive. The process was extremely painful and could kill young girls if an infection set in. Once bound, the feet could hardly hold a person's weight, confining women to the household. Walking very far was just too painful and awkward. Yet even though the Manchu declared it illegal, upper-class Chinese families continued the practice.

More successful were Manchu attempts to end widow suicide. Confucian ideals emphasized loyalty of a person lower in rank to the person above—for example, of a child to parents, and of a wife to a husband. Under the Ming, a cult of widow suicide had grown in which a widow killed herself when her husband died. Kangxi attacked widow suicide as "cowardly." It took more courage, he claimed, to live and support the family. As a later emperor, Qianlong, pointed out, "Sometimes wives and daughters originally do not want to die but are pressured by husbands or parents to do so." To counter this practice, he ordered the restoration of Buddhist temples dedicated to

Kuanyin, a female deity believed to comfort as a mother or grandmother might do. This image of a sympathetic older woman still useful to her family helped to eliminate the cult of widow suicide.

The emperor's symbols, a dragon with five claws, flames, clouds, and a pearl, decorate the imperial seal of Kangxi. A conscientious reader of state documents, Kangxi's seal was more than just an empty stamp of approval.

Although the Manchu tried to keep their own values, they also recognized that they were vastly outnumbered by the Chinese and had to respect Chinese culture. Unlike some empire leaders, they followed a practice of bringing their enemies over to them. For example, in war with the Ming, they often negotiated with Ming generals, promising them commands if they switched sides. For the most part, the Chinese did not often see Manchu troops, which kept the Chinese from feeling resentment toward their rulers. Most of the Manchu troops were kept north, and Chinese troops loyal to the Manchu were used throughout the empire. Through their partial embrace of Confucian ideas and support of Buddhist shrines, the Manchus maintained the illusion that Chinese culture was intact. In Tibet, Outer Mongolia, Korea, and Central Asia as well, the Manchu did not pressure the population to change religious practices or interfere with long-held local customs.

Manchu policies, for the most part, were successful in holding China together, particularly in the first 150 years of Manchu rule. There was, however, Ming resistance. Ming loyalist poets, such as Ch'en Ch'en Yi, used imagery to protest. His poem "Watching a Game of Chess" contains phrases such as "hollow echoes," "the cold tide," "white head," and "a dying game of chess." The best, he implies, has passed. Many historians would, however, disagree with his view of the times. Kangxi and Qianlong each ruled for more than 60 years and provided stability for China.

THE CELESTIAL SUNS: KANGXI AND QIANLONG

The life and rule of Kangxi probably best illustrates the balance between the best of Manchu and Chinese values. Orphaned by seven, he grew tall, even tempered, and forever curious. He took seriously the Confucian idea that a

"There's an old saying that if the civilian officers don't seek money and the military officials aren't afraid of death, we need never fear that the country won't have Great Peace."

—Kangxi, second Qing emperor, document in Qing archives, about 1711

ruler's duty was to bring welfare to the people. He was also straightforward. When in 1672, a general reported that "the rebel supplies are low and they are ready to surrender," Kangxi tried to pin him down. How many rebels, what supplies, how far away? The general had to admit there were quite a few rebels, actually, and there would be battles ahead. Kangxi toured the provinces, examining, for example, the dike system on the Yangzi River, and he took a hands-on approach in the Chinese examination system, at times writing out questions and grading the upper-level papers himself.

The Manchu realized that trouble was most likely to come from the scholar class in China, who might subvert them, so the emperors kept scholars busy. Kangxi and a growing school of *Kaozheng* (hard facts) scholars tried to salvage Chinese history by publishing a book called *History of the Ming Dynasty*, an encyclopedia, dictionary, and literary anthology all in one.

A good Confucian ruler was to be concerned with the peasants and the deserving poor. In keeping with that belief, Kangxi asked his advisors whether peasants and landlords were paying fair and equal shares of taxes. He also had a sense that justice could be complicated. When bandits were put down, Kangxi wrote the War Board, "Spare the others. . . . the children must be spared. . . . The women in the bandits' camps were often initially taken there by force. . . . so let the . . . local people have a chance to identify and reclaim the refugees and their children—don't arrest everyone."

Kangxi did have one major failure; his heir apparent, his eldest son Yinreng, turned out to be dishonest, untrustworthy, and arrogant. Kangxi tried all sorts of threats, bribes, and removals of privileges, but his son's behavior did not change, and he finally imprisoned him. The final blow came when Yinreng intercepted some imperial horses that were being sent to the Mongols and kept them for his own. Everyone knew you didn't mess with Mongols and their horses.

After Kangxi's death in 1725 and a brief rule by one of his sons, Kangxi's grandson Qianlong took over. Qianlong tried to model himself after Kangxi, but he did not have the same sense of balance that his grandfather had. "Bigger and Better" might have been his slogan. Emulating his grandfather's efforts in producing *The History of the Ming*, Qianlong had his scholars publish the Library of the Four Treasuries of Confucian Classics, a monumental collection of 36,000 books and another 79,582 volumes of Chinese history, philosophy, and literature. But works criticizing the Manchu were destroyed. Qianlong also had paintings collected and brought to the palace at China's northern capital, Beijing.

During one of his royal tours in 1699, Emperor Kangxi showed interest in both his lands and his capable army. Kangxi's frequent tours were one way to avoid potential problems. As he wrote, "Stirring up trouble is not as good as preventing trouble from happening."

Built in 1405, the Forbidden City in Beijing is one of the greatest palaces in the world. The center of the Chinese empire for 500 years, the complex contains almost 9,000 rooms, accessible to the rest of Beijing by four monumental gateways.

This act probably helped preserve some of the more than 10,000 works brought to the palace. But these paintings were also withdrawn from public view, and painters generally could not study them for inspiration or technique.

Like his grandfather, Qianlong wanted to expand the borders of China, though he did not go campaigning himself. Instead, he sent General Zhaohui into Central Asia in 1757, along the Silk Road, to capture an area from Dunhuang to the Pamir Mountains (in present-day Tajikistan), which made China larger than it would ever be again. Zhaohui and his troops suffered frostbite, starvation, thirst, and even cannibalism in probably the most horrible Manchu campaign. When Zhaohui returned, Qianlong did him the honor of greeting him outside the palace gates.

At midcentury, in 1750, Qianlong could survey much of China and feel that the first Manchu rulers had done well. The population, fed by new lands and new crops such as corn, sweet potatoes, and peanuts, seemed in better health and was growing. Chinese porcelain, silk, and artwork were bringing in huge amounts of silver to the treasury and merchants' pockets. But in the next part of his reign, Qianlong lost his direction and relied on a corrupt Manchu noble to

"Every. . . ruler, when he has returned from audience, and has finished his public duties, must have a garden in which he may stroll, look around and relax his heart. If he has a suitable place for this it will refresh his mind and regularize his emotions."

—Qianlong, fourth Qing emperor, document in Qing archives, 1740s run the government. Foreigners from Europe, with more advanced technology, pressured China for trade. Kangxi may have understood this reversal of fortune. In studying the Chinese classic *Book of Changes*, he was especially fond of the following passage: "When the sun stands at midday, it begins to set, when the moon is full, it begins to wane. The fullness and emptiness of heaven and earth wane and wax in the course of time. How much truer is this of men."

Manchu power withered in the next century and a half, until the Manchu were overthrown in 1912.

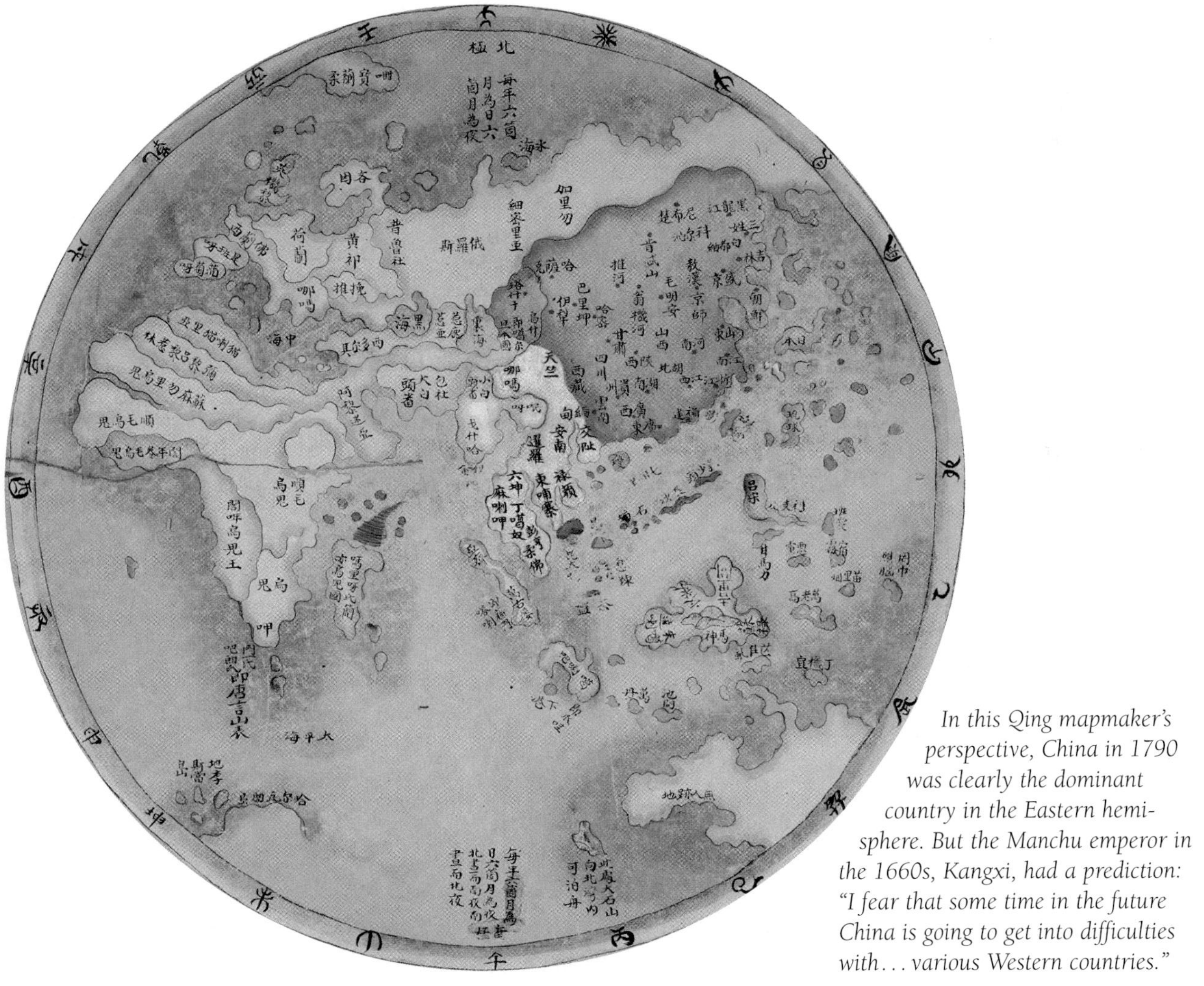

In this Qing mapmaker's perspective, China in 1790 was clearly the dominant country in the Eastern hemisphere. But the Manchu emperor in the 1660s, Kangxi, had a prediction: "I fear that some time in the future China is going to get into difficulties with . . . various Western countries."

EPILOGUE

REMEMBERING THE CONQUESTS

In 1793, King George III of England, having lost the American colonies, was looking for new places to trade with. A major trading embassy was sent to China to open up more ports for English products. After all, the English bought many goods from China. Tea imports alone had gone from five chests, in 1684, to nearly 23 million pounds by the 1790s. The Qing emperor Qianlong tolerated his British visitors for a while, but finally told them to go home: "Our Celestial Empire possesses all things in prolific abundance and lacks no product within its own borders. There was, therefore, no need to import the manufactures of outside barbarians in exchange for our own produce."

Qianlong was wrong about how little China needed the "outside world"; the connections with other cultures had already been made. From the Mongols, the Manchu had learned military tactics and how to control vast territories. The Qing calendar and Qing astronomers were, thanks to Western Jesuit scientists, using the ideas of Poland's Copernicus and the mathematical planetary tables of the Habsburg's Johannes Kepler. From India came ideas about Buddhism; in Kangxi's grandmother's last portrait, she is dressed as a Buddhist nun. Those Silk Road cities of the "New Territories" would not have been worth taking if the Ottomans in Istanbul did not buy goods and send their rugs, glassware, and jewelry along the road to China. Spain's empire had distributed new American plants around the world. Corn grew on Chinese lands too rugged and dry for rice. Sweet potatoes and peanuts added nutrition to the diet of the poor, and more survived, to raise China's population. Jesuit priests, their order founded in Spain by Ignatius Loyola, served in the Manchu court. The summer palace of Yanmingyuan was designed for Qianlong by Jesuit architects in a Western style. At the Portuguese center in China at Macao, all sorts of goods were exchanged. Kang Shangren, a Qing poet, even wrote about one: "White glass from across the Western Seas is imported through Macao. Fashioned into lenses big as coins. . . . I put them on—it suddenly becomes clear."

All of the empires connected people in new ways. But human costs were high, not just in the battles so frequently fought. Singde, a Manchu soldier, wrote a poem in the mid-17th century about going to the Russian border to face, what he assumed would be, more battles:

Cold and silent, the dew deep in the night;
The crows unsteady, perching in the
winter wind
How I hate the insistent battle drum from
the tower
That keeps a soldier from returning—even
in dreams!
Drab autumn, A crescent moon,
No one gets up to gaze into its depths
At dawn a horse will take me on, another
place—the same longing
If you knew how many mountains are
rising between us!

Emperor Qianlong sits in the position of a Bodhisattva, or holy one in the Buddhist faith. Jesuit missionaries, such as the painter, compared the grandeur of Qianlong's court to that of the French king Louis XV.

The world from 1200 to 1750 was linked by empires. We study empires to understand how our ideas about science and literature came to be; where we got our sweet potatoes and our not-so-sweet villains; how it felt to set out on adventure; and the price of defeats. We also study empires to puzzle out our own judgments on what it means to be human on a larger scale than just ourselves. There's adventure in that as well.

GLOSSARY

ablution washing for the sake of purification

Assassins Islamic group known for its treachery that resisted the Mongols

boyars (BOY-yahrs) Russian nobles

conquistadors (kon-KEES-tah-dohrs) leaders of the Spanish conquest of America in the 16th century

converso (kon-VEHR-so) Spanish word for Jews who converted to Christianity

cuius regio, eius religio (COO-yoos REE-gee-o AYE-oos ree-LIH-gee-oh) Latin phrase meaning the religion of the ruler would determine his subjects' religion

deluge a severe and destructive storm; also a name for a period of decline for Poland and Lithuania in the 17th and 18th centuries

dominion power or right to rule

devshirme (dehv-sheer-MEH) Ottoman sultans' system for recruiting non-Muslim boys to train as personal servants and soldiers, from the Turkish word meaning "harvest"

dhimmis (THIHM-ihs) people of the Book; Ottoman name for Jews and Christians

Domonstroi (doh-muh-STROY) Russian religious document that said women should be completely submissive to their husbands

gers (gurhz) round tents used by the Mongols

harem a separate, hidden part of a house for Muslim women

heretic a person who does not believe in accepted religious thought

heretical relating to a departure from accepted beliefs

Iberian Peninsula (aye-BEER-ee-an) the peninsula making up Portugal and Spain

icon a representation of a sacred person, often painted on wood

infidel someone who is seen as opposing accepted religious views

jizya (JEEZ-yah) in the Mughal empire, a tax on non-Muslims

Kanun-i-Osman (kah-NOON-ee-OHS-mahn) the term for laws in the Ottoman Empire

kuruc (KOOR-oots) Hungarian freedom fighters

Ladies' Peace a peace agreement that Margaret of Parma, a Habsburg, negotiated with the French duchess Louise of Savoy on behalf of their countries

magnate a large landholder in Poland and Lithuania

mercenary a soldier paid to serve in a foreign army

minaret (mih-nah-REHT) slender towers attached to a mosque

moriscos (muh-RIHS-kos) Muslims living in Spain who converted to Christianity during the Inquisition

nomad member of a group of people without a permanent home

oprichniki (ah-PREECH-nee-kee) a secret police that Ivan the Terrible established in Russia

pax (packs) the Latin word for peace

Pax Mongolica (packs mohn-GOH-lee-ah) trade from China to the Mediterranean in the Mongol Empire

Pax Romana (packs roh-MAH-nah) road system and trade in the Roman Empire

qurittai (KUHR-ih-tie) a gathering of Mongols where a ruler would be chosen

Reformation 16th-century revolt against the Catholic Church that led to Protestantism

shaman (SHAH-man) Mongolian religious leader

Shi'a (SHEE-ah) a Muslim sect that differs from the Sunni by believing that descendants of the prophet Mohammed should lead Islam

siege engine large war machines used to attack fortifications

steppe large, flat, treeless areas of land in southeastern Europe or Asia

strelsty (struhl-TSE) musketeers of the Russian Army who joined the peasants to revolt against the Romanovs

sultan (SOOL-tahn) Turkish ruler

szlachta (SHLAHK-tah) Polish word for the gentry who elected the Polish king

terem (TEH-rehm) a secluded part of a home where upper-class Russian women stayed

tsar (zahr) Russian ruler

Ulema (oo-lehm-AH) the leaders of the Islamic court system within the Ottoman Empire

valide sultan (vah-lee-DAY SOOL-tahn) mother of the sultan, or ruler, an important position

veni, vidi, deus vincit (VEH-ni VEE-dee DAY-us VIHN-siht) Latin phrase meaning "I came, I saw, God conquered."

victuals food supplies

vizier (vih-ZEER) top Turkish administrative official

yarlick (yahr-LUK) a slice of tax collection money rewarded to Russian princes who worked for the Mongols

TIMELINE

1071
Seljuk Turks defeat Byzantine Army at Manzikert

around 1155
Temujin (Genghis Khan) is born

1206
Genghis Khan becomes Mongol leader

1220
Mongols take over Silk Road cities of Bukhara and Samarkand

1223
Russian lose to Mongols at Battle of Kalka

1227
Genghis Khan dies; his sons continue Mongolian Empire

1240
Mongols sack Kiev

1264
Khubilai Khan makes a capital at Beijing and begins Yuan dynasty

1281
Khubilai Khan tries to attack Japan but is unsuccessful

1396
Yuan dynasty ends and Ming dynasty takes over China

1370
Timur the Lame captures Samarkand and makes it his empire's capital

1380
Russians defeat Golden Horde at Kulikovo

1386
Jogaila and Jadwiga marry and unite Poland and Lithuania

1387
Ottomans defeat Serbs at Kosovo

1410
Poles and Lithuanians defeat Teutonic Knights at Tannenberg

1415
Jan Hus is burnt as a heretic for his writing on religious reform

1453
Ottomans defeat Byzantines and take over Constantinople

1492
Isabella and Ferdinand defeat Muslims at Granada; Isabella and Ferdinand give orders that all Jews must leave Spain; Isabella provides funds for Columbus's voyage; Columbus reaches America

1497–1499
Vasco da Gama voyages around Africa to East Indies

1513
Portuguese explore coast of Brazil, reach China

1519
Magellan sets sail to circumnavigate the world; Cortés sets out for Mexico

1520
Margaret of Netherlands and Louise of Savoy negotiate "Ladies Peace"

1526
Babur takes over northern India at Battle of Panipat; Turks win at Mohacs

1543
Copernicus publishes *On the Revolution of the Heavenly Spheres*

1555
Catholics and Lutherans agree to Treaty of Augsburg, which says the ruler can determine a nation's religion

1556
Akbar consolidates power in second Battle of Panipat

1566
Suleyman the Magnificent dies, ending Ottoman Golden Age

1571
Charles V's navy defeats Turks in Battle of Lepanto

1584
Ivan the Terrible dies and Russia's Time of Troubles begins

1588
Philip II attacks Elizabeth I of England with Spanish Armada

1618
Thirty Years' War begins

1620
Habsburgs defeat Bohemian forces at White Mountain

1644
Manchus move into China and begin Qing dynasty

1648
Thirty Years' War ends with Treaty of Westphalia

1661
Kangxi begins successful reign in China

1676
Alexis dies; Peter the Great, Ivan IV, and regent Sophia share power

1683
Ottomans attack Vienna and are defeated by army led by Jan Sobieski

1688
Spain recognizes Portugal's independence

1697
Manchu take Outer Mongolia

1703
War of Spanish Succession begins

1709
Russians defeat Swedes in Battle of Poltava

1725
Peter the Great dies after instituting major reforms

1740
Maria Theresa inherits Habsburg throne; Frederick attacks Silesia

1757
Lisbon earthquake

FURTHER READING

Entries with [“] indicate primary source material.

GENERAL WORKS ON EMPIRES AND EARLY MODERN HISTORY

Davis, Mary Lee. *Women Who Changed History: Five Famous Queens of Europe.* Minneapolis: Lerner, 1975.

Meltzer, Milton. *Ten Kings and the Worlds They Ruled.* New York: Orchard, 2002.

———. *Ten Queens: Portraits of Women of Power.* New York: Dutton, 1998.

ATLASES

Adams, Simon, et al. *Illustrated Atlas of World History.* New York: Random House, 1992.

Barnes, Ian. *The History Atlas of Europe.* New York: Macmillan, 1998.

Channon, John. *The Penguin Historical Atlas of Russia.* New York: Penguin, 1995.

Davies, Philip. *The History Atlas of North America.* New York: Macmillan, 1998.

Early, Edwin. *The History Atlas of South America.* New York: Macmillan, 1998.

Farrington, Karen. *Historical Atlas of Empires.* New York: Checkmark, 2002.

Haywood, John. *World Atlas of the Past,* 4 vols. New York: Oxford University Press, 1999.

Hupchick, Dennis P. *A Concise Historical Atlas of Eastern Europe.* New York: St. Martin's, 1996.

O'Brien, Patrick K., ed. *Atlas of World History.* New York: Oxford University Press, 1999.

Pogonowski, Iwo. *Poland, A Historical Atlas.* New York: Hippocrene, 1987.

DICTIONARIES AND ENCYCLOPEDIAS

Dewald, Jonathan, ed. *Europe 1450 to 1789: Encyclopedia of the Early Modern World.* New York: Charles Scribner's Sons, 2004.

Stearns, Peter N., and William L. Langer, eds. *The Encyclopedia of World History.* Boston: Houghton Mifflin, 2001.

BIOGRAPHY

See biographies under the heading for each empire.

THE HABSBURG EMPIRE

Ingrao, Charles W. *The Habsburg Monarchy, 1618–1915.* New York; Cambridge University Press, 2000.

Okey, Robin. *The Habsburg Monarchy: From Enlightenment to Eclipse.* New York: St. Martin's, 2001.

[“] Pick, Robert. *Empress Maria Theresa: The Earlier Years, 1717–1757.* New York: Harper and Row, 1966.

Voelkel, James R. *Johannes Kepler and the New Astronomy.* New York: Oxford University Press, 2001.

THE MANCHU EMPIRE

Crossley, Pamela Kyle. *Orphan Warriors: Three Manchu Generations and the End of the Qing World.* Princeton, N.J.: Princeton University Press, 1990.

Hoff, Rhoda. *China: Adventures in Eyewitness History.* New York: Walck, 1965.

Hoobler, Dorothy, and Thomas Hoobler. *Chinese Portraits.* Austin, Tex.: Raintree Steck-Vaughn, 1993.

Mann, Elizabeth. *The Great Wall.* New York: Mikaya Press, 1997.

Naquin, Susan. *Peking: Temples and City Life, 1400–1900.* Berkeley: University of California Press, 2000.

Roberson, John R. *China from Manchu to Mao (1699–1976).* New York: Atheneum, 1980.

Yutang, Ling, ed. *The Wisdom of China and India*. New York: Modern Library, 1941.

THE MONGOL EMPIRE

Cohen, Daniel. *Conquerors on Horseback*. New York: Doubleday, 1970.

Greenblatt, Miriam. *Genghis Khan and the Mongol Empire*. New York: Benchmark, 2002.

Humphrey, Judy. *Genghis Khan*. New York: Chelsea House, 1987.

Nicolle, David. *The Mongol Warlords*. Dorset, U.K.: Firebird, 1990.

Onon, Urgunger, trans. *The Golden History of the Mongols: Genghis Khan*. London: Folio Society, 1993

Polo, Marco. *The Travels of Marco Polo: For Boys and Girls*. New York: Putnam, 1988.

Roux, Jean-Paul. *Genghis Khan and the Mongol Empire*. New York: Abrams, 2003.

Taylor, Robert. *Life in Genghis Khan's Mongolia*. San Diego, Calif.: Lucent, 2001.

Weatherford, Jack. *Genghis Khan and the Making of the Modern World*. New York: Crown, 2004.

Worth, Richard. *The Great Empire of China and Marco Polo in World History*. Berkeley Heights, N.J.: Enslow, 2003.

THE MUGHAL EMPIRE

Beach, Milo Cleveland. *The Imperial Image: Paintings for the Mughal Court*. Washington, D.C.: Freer Gallery of Art, Smithsonian Institution, 1981.

Bérinstain, Valérie. *India and the Mughal Dynasty*. New York: Abrams, 1998.

Brand, Michael. *Akbar's India: Art from the Mughal City of Victory*. New York: Asia Society Galleries, 1985.

DuTemple, Lesley A. *The Taj Mahal*. Minneapolis: Lerner, 2003.

Rothfarb, Ed. *In the Land of the Taj Mahal*. New York: Henry Holt, 1998

Skelton, Robert, et al. *The Indian Heritage: Court Life and Arts under Mughal Rule*. New York: Universe, 1982.

Tillotson, G. H. R. *Mughal India*. San Francisco: Chronicle, 1990.

Welch, Stuart Cary, et al. *The Emperors' Album: Images of Mughal India*. New York: Metropolitan Museum of Art/Abrams, 1987.

THE OTTOMAN EMPIRE

Addison, John. *Suleyman and the Ottoman Empire*. San Diego: Greenhaven, 1986.

Atil, Esin. *The Age of Sultan Suleyman the Magnificent*. Washington, D.C.: National Gallery of Art, 1987.

Barbir, Karl K. *Ottoman Rule in Damascus, 1708–1758*. Princeton, N.J.: Princeton University Press, 1980.

Celebi, Eviya. *The Intimate Life of an Ottoman Statesman, Malek Ahmed Pasha 1558–1662*. Trans. and commentary by Robert Dankoff. Albany: State University of New York Press, 1991.

Corrick, James. *The Byzantine Empire*. San Diego, Calif..: Lucent, 1997.

Goodwin, Jason. *Lords of the Horizons: A History of the Ottoman Empire*. New York: Henry Holt, 1999.

Greenblatt, Miriam. *Suleyman the Magnificent and the Ottoman Empire*. New York: Benchmark, 2002.

Roberts, J. M. *The Age of Diverging Traditions*. New York: Oxford University Press, 2001.

Ruggiero, Adriane. *The Ottoman Empire*. New York: Benchmark, 2003.

Wheatcroft, Andrew. *The Ottomans*. New York: Viking, 1993.

THE POLISH AND LITHUANIAN EMPIRES

Andronik, Catherine M. *Copernicus: Founder of Modern Astronomy*. Berkeley Heights, N.J.: Enslow, 2002.

Gingerich, Owen, and James MacLachlan. *Nicolaus Copernicus: Making the Earth a Planet*. New York: Oxford University Press, 2005.

Hintz, Martin. *Poland.* New York: Children's Press, 1998.

Kagda, Sakina. *Lithuania.* New York: Marshall Cavendish, 1997.

THE PORTUGUESE EMPIRE

Anderson, James Maxwell. *The History of Portugal.* Westport, Conn.: Greenwood, 2000.

Burnside, Madeline. *Spirit of Passage: The Transatlantic Slave Trade in the Seventeenth Century.* New York: Simon & Schuster, 1997.

Chubb, Thomas Caldecot. *Prince Henry the Navigator and the Highways of the Sea.* New York: Viking, 1970.

Goodman, Joan Elizabeth. *A Long and Uncertain Journey: The 27,000 Mile Voyage of Vasco da Gama.* New York: Mikaya, 2001.

Palmer, Colin. *The First Passage: Blacks in the Americas 1502–1617.* New York: Oxford University Press, 1995.

Thomas, Hugh. *The Slave Trade: the Story of the Aatlantic Slave Trade, 1440–1870.* New York: Touchstone, 1997.

THE RUSSIAN EMPIRE

Butson, Thomas G. *Ivan the Terrible.* New York: Chelsea House, 1987.

Cracraft, James. *The Revolution of Peter the Great.* Cambridge, Mass.: Harvard University Press, 2003.

Guillaume Le Vasseu, Sieur de Bauplan. *A Description of Ukraine, containing several provinces of the kingdom of Poland, lying between the confines of Muscovy...* London, 1744.

Hughes, Lindsey. *Russia in the Age of Peter the Great.* New Haven, Conn.: Yale University Press, 1998.

———. *Peter the Great: A Biography.* New Haven, Conn.: Yale University Press, 2002.

Kort, Michael. *Russia.* New York: Facts on File, 1995.

Murrell, Kathleen Berton. *Russia.* New York: Dorling Kindersley, 2000.

Stanley, Diane. *Peter the Great.* New York: Morrow, 1999.

Strickler, Jim. *Russia of the Tsars.* San Diego, Calif.: Lucent, 1998.

THE SPANISH EMPIRE

Baquedano, Elizabeth. *Aztec, Inca and Maya.* New York: Dorling Kindersley, 1993.

Barghusen, Joan. *The Aztecs.* San Diego: Lucent, 1999.

Burch, Joann J. *Isabella of Castile: Queen on Horseback.* New York: Franklin Watts, 1991.

Diaz del Castillo, Bernal. *Cortez and the Conquest of Mexico by the Spaniards in 1521: Being the Eye-witness Narrative of Bernal Diaz del Castillo, Soldier of Fortune and Conquistador with Cortez in Mexico.* B. G. Herzog, ed. Hamden, Conn.: Linnet, 1988.

Flowers, Charles. *Cortés and the Conquest of the Aztec Empire in World History.* Berkeley Heights, N.J.: Enslow, 2001.

Kamen, Henry Arthur Francis. *Empire: How Spain Became a World Power, 1492–1763.* New York: HarperCollins, 2003.

Levinson, Nancy Smiler. *Magellan and the First Voyage around the World.* New York: Clarion, 2001.

Lilley, Stephen. *The Conquest of Mexico.* San Diego, Calif.: Lucent, 1997.

Maestro, Betsy, and Giulio Maestro. *Exploration and Conquest: The Americas after Columbus 1500–1620.* New York: Mulberry, 1997.

Marrin, Albert. *Aztecs and Spaniards: Cortés and the Conquest of Mexico.* New York: Atheneum, 1986.

Stevens, Paul. *Ferdinand and Isabella.* New York: Chelsea House, 1988.

Thomas, Hugh. *Rivers of Gold: The Rise of the Spanish Empire, from Columbus to Magellan.* New York: Random House, 2003.

West, Delno C., and Jean M. West. *Christopher Columbus: The Great Adventure and How We Know About It.* New York: Atheneum, 1991.

Worth, Richard. *The Spanish Inquisition in World History.* Berkeley Heights, N.J.: Enslow, 2002.

WEBSITES

THE HABSBURG EMPIRE

Maria Theresa, Archduchess of Austria
www.kings.edu/womens_history/mariatheres.html
Created by the King's College department of history, this webpage consists of a short biography and an annotated bibliography for this Habsburg monarch.

MONGOLS

Legacy of Genghis Khan
www.metmuseum.org/toah/hd/khan1/hd_khan1.htm
Artwork from the Metropolitan Museum related to Mongols in Iran, China, and Russia, plus timelines and maps.

The Mongols in World History
http://afe.easia.columbia.edu/mongols/
Responds to questions about Mongol conquests, influences and way of life.

The Silkroad Foundation
www.silk-road.com/toc/index.html
Art, maps, chronologies, and many informative links related to the Silk Road

MUGHALS

Art of the Mughals before 1600 A.D.
www.metmuseum.org/toah/hd/mugh/hd_mugh.htm
Paintings and architecture from the Metropolian Museum illustrate the skill of Mughal artists

World Civilizations: The Mughals
www.wsu.edu:8080/~dee/MUGHAL/CONTENTS.HTM
Washington State University's internet classroom provides information on Mughal history and rulers, including a glossary of terms and a gallery of art and architecture.

THE OTTOMAN EMPIRE

Sultans: The 700th Anniversary of the Ottoman Empire
www.osmanli700.gen.tr/english/sultans/10index.html
General illustrated site for Ottoman history with extensive background information on 36 sultans including Selim and Suleyman.

World Civilizations: The Ottomans
www.wsu.edu:8080/~dee/OTTOMAN/ORIGIN.HTM
Offers a tour of numerous topics relating to the Ottomans, particularly Suleyman.

POLAND AND LITHUANIA

About.com European History/Poland
http://europeanhistory.about.com/cs/poland
Annotated list of websites relating to Polish history, documents, and maps.

The ORB: The Teutonic Order
www.the-orb.net/encyclop/religion/monastic/opsahl1.html
Describes the origin, structure and expansion of the Teutonic Order and includes a timeline and a selected bibliography.

THE PORTUGUESE AND SPANISH EMPIRES

Africans in America: Prince Henry the Navigator
www.pbs.org/wgbh/aia/part1/1p259.html
Based on the public television series *Africans in America*, the site contains original sources and illustrations describing early Portuguese encounters with Africans.

The Columbus Navigation Homepage
www1.minn.net/~keithp/
Details Columbus's voyages, his ships and crew, and the navigational methods practiced in the 16th century.

Discovers Web: Henry the Navigator
www.win.tue.nl/cs/fm/engels/discovery/henry.html
Summarizes Henry's life and provides links to a number of good websites about Portuguese exploration.

RUSSIA

Florida International Museum: Treasures of the Czars
www2.sptimes.com/Treasures/
A timeline of rulers, fun facts, and online art from the reign of Peter and other tsars showing Western influences.

Modern History Sourcebook: Peter the Great and the Rise of Russia, 1682–1725
www.fordham.edu/halsall/mod/petergreat.html
Foreigners' firsthand accounts of Peter's reign.

INDEX

References to illustrations and their captions are indicated by page numbers in **bold**.

TEXT AND PICTURE CREDITS

TEXT CREDITS

P. 14: "The Letter of Andrew of Perugia," in *The Mongol Mission,* ed. Christopher Dawson (New York: Sheed and Ward, 1955), 237.

P. 15: *The Golden History of the Mongols: Genghis Khan,* trans. Urgunge Onon (London: Folio Society, 1993), 111.

P. 20: William of Rubruck, *The Mission of Friar William of Rubruck,* trans. Peter Jackson (London: Hukluyt Society, 1990), 131.

P. 22: Ala-ad-Din Ata-Malik Juvaini, *The History of the World Conqueror,* trans. John Andrew Boyle, vol. 1, 152, in Morris Rossabi, *Khubilai Khan* (Berkeley: University of California Press, 1988), 2.

P. 25:*The Golden History of the Mongols: Genghis Khan,* trans. Urgunge Onon (London: The Folio Society, 1993), 139–40.

P. 28: Polo, Marco, *The Travels of Marco Polo,* ed. Manuel Komroff (New York: W. W. Norton, 1926), 136–39.

P. 31: Prawdin, Michael, (pseud. Michael Charol), *The Mongol Empire: Its Rise and Legacy* (London: Allen and Unwin, 1952), 452.

P. 33: *Koryo sa,* vol. 110:23b–25b, in *Sources of Korean Tradition,* vol. 1, ed. Peter H. Lee and William Theodore de Bary (New York: Columbia University Press, 1997), 203.

P. 34: Hoang, Michel, *Genghis Khan,* trans. Ingrid Cranfield (New York: New Amsterdam, 1990), 192.

P. 39: Dlugosz, Jan, *The Annals of Jan Dlugosz,* English abridgement by Maurice Michael (Chichester, England: IM Publications, 1997), 391.

P. 41: Davies, Norman, *God's Playground: A History of Poland,* vol. 1 (New York: Columbia University Press, 1982), 244.

P. 42: Copernicus, Nicholas, *On the Revolution of the Heavenly Spheres,* in John Henry, *Moving Heaven and Earth: Copernicus and the Solar System* (Duxford, England: Icon, 2001), 53.

P. 44: Guillaume Le Vasseu, Sieur de Bauplan, *A Description of Ukraine, containing several provinces of the kingdom of Poland, lying between the confines of Muscovy...* (London, 1744), 603–4.

P. 45:Dlugosz, Jan, *The Annals of Jan Dlugosz,* English abridgement Michael, 428.

P. 52: Hughes, Lindsey, *Russia in the Age of Peter the Great* (New Haven: Yale University Press, 1998), 416.

P. 54: Kelly, Laurence, *Moscow: A Travellers' Companion* (New York: Antheneum, 1984), 36.

P. 57: *Diary of an Austrian Secretary of Legation at the Court of Czar Peter the Great,* in Anthony Cross, ed., *Russia under Western Eyes 1517–1825* (New York: St. Martin's Press, 1971), 146.

P. 59: Longworth, Philip, *Alexis, Tsar of All the Russias* (New York: Franklin Watts, 1984), 9.

P. 63: Eraly, Abraham, *The Last Spring: The Lives and Times of the Great Mughals* (New York: Viking, 1997), 403.

P. 65: Bernier, François, *Travels in the Mogul Empire,* (Delhi: S. Chand, 1968), 272–3.

P. 67: Eraly, *The Last Spring,* 139.

P. 68: Hansen, Waldemar, *The Peacock Throne: The Drama of Mogul India* (Delhi: Motilal Banarsidass Publishers, 1972), 68.

P. 70: Eraly, *The Last Spring,* 663.

P. 73: Andric, Ivo, *The Development of Spiritual Life in Bosnia under the Influence of Turkish Rule* (Durham, N.C.: Duke University Press, 1990), 37.

P. 75: Mansel, Philip, *Constantinople* (New York: St. Martin's Press, 1996), 17.

P. 78: Clot, Andrei, *Suleiman the Magnificent,* (New York: New Amsterdam, 1992), 39.

P. 81: Celebi, Evliya, *The Intimate Life of an Ottoman Statesman, Melek Ahmed Pasha 1558–1662,* trans. and commentary by Robert Dankoff (Albany: State University of New York Press, 1991), 226, 234.

P. 82: Vryonis, Speros, *Byzantium and Europe* (New York: Harcourt, Brace, 1967), 190.

P. 86: Bridge, Anthony, *Suleiman the Magnificent* (New York: Dorset, 1966), 203.

P. 89: Hale, John, *The Civilization of Europe in the Renaissance* (New York: Atheneum, 1994), 40.

P. 90: Barbir, Karl K., *Ottoman Rule in Damascus, 1708–1758* (Princeton, N.J.: Princeton University Press, 1980), 112–13.

P. 92: Lady Mary Wrotley Montague, *Embassy to Constantinople* (New York: New Amsterdam, 1988), 174.

P. 94: Miller, Louis, *Ottoman Turkish Writers* (New York: Peter Lang, 1988), 35.

P. 99: Russell-Wood, A. J. R., *The Portuguese Empire 1415–1808* (Baltimore: Johns Hopkins University Press, 1992), 221.

P. 104: Thomas, Hugh, *The Slave Trade: The Story of the Atlantic Slave Trade: 1440–1870* (New York: Touchstone, 1997), 21–22.

P. 105: Boxer, Charles, *The Portuguese Seaborne Empire 1415–1825* (New York: Knopf, 1969), 153.

P. 111: Kamen, Henry, *Empire: How Spain Became a World Power 1492–1763* (New York: Harper Collins, 2003), 286.

P. 113: Graham, Robert, *The Conquest of the River Plate* (New York: Greenwood, 1924), 281–84.

P. 115: Thomas, Hugh, *Rivers of Gold: The Rise of the Spanish Empire, from Columbus to Magellan* (New York: Random House, 2003), 219.

P. 116: Thomas, *Rivers of Gold,* 294.

P. 119: Crow, John A., *Spain: The Root and the Flower* (Berkeley: University of California Press, 1985), 153.

P. 122: Ferguson, Kitty, *Tycho and Kepler* (New York: Walker, 2002), 155.

P. 127: Pick, Robert, *Empress Maria Theresa: The Earlier Years, 1717–1757* (New York: Harper and Row, 1966), 73–74.

P. 129: Langer, Herbert, *The Thirty Years' War* (New York: Dorset, 1978).

P. 131: Tapie, Victor-L., *The Rise and Fall of the Habsburg Monarchy* (London: Pall Mall, 1971), 60.

P. 135: Yutang, Lin, ed., *The Wisdom of China and India* (New York: Modern Library, 1941), 1070–71.

P. 140: Spence, Jonathan D., *Emperor of China: Self-portrait of Kang-hsi* (New York: Vintage, 1988), 56.

P. 142: Smith, Richard J., *China's Cultural Heritage: The Qing Dynasty, 1644–1912* (Boulder, Colo.: Westview, 1994), 199.

PICTURE CREDITS

Adam Lubroth / Art Resource, NY: 110; Archives du Ministere des Affaires Etrangeres, Paris / The Bridgeman Art Library: 125; Private Collection, Ancient Art and Architecture Collection Ltd / The Bridgeman Art Library: 33; Art and History Collection. Photography courtesy of the Arthur M. Sackler Gallery, Smithsonian Institution, Washington, D.C. LTS1995.2.9.: cover Spine; Art Museum of Kostroma, Russia / The Bridgeman Art Library: 58; Art Museum of Yaroslavl, Russia / The Bridgeman Art Library: 49; Art Resource, NY: 18,24, 90; Biblioteca Nacional, Madrid / The Bridgeman Art Library: 116; Bibliotheque nationale de France: 101; Bibliotheque Nationale de France, Paris, France / The Bridgeman Art Library: 26; Bildarchiv Preussischer Kulturbesitz / Art Resource, NY: 124, 143; Bridgeman-Giraudon / Art Resource, NY: 12, 72, 83, 93, 106, 120; British Library, London / The Bridgeman Art Library: 74, 141; The British Museum, London / The Bridgeman Art Library: 35; © The Trustees of the British Museum: 13, 86; Capilla Real, Granada / The Bridgeman Art Library: 107; Castilla-La Mancha, Toledo / The Bridgeman Art Library: 118; Erich Lessing / Art Resource, NY: 40, 43, 76, 85, 128, 130, 132; Foto Marburg / Art Resource, NY: 82; Freer Gallery of Art, Smithsonian Institution, Washington D.C.: Gift of Charles Langer Freer, F1909.231:137, Purchase F1954.3.1: 36, Purchase, F1954.29: 71, Purchase—Anonymous donor and Museum Funds, F200.4: 145; Kunsthistorisches Museum, Wien oder KHM, Wien: 77; Ex.coll: C.C. Wang Family, The Metropolitan Museum of Art, Gift of the Dillion Fund, 1973 (1973.120.7a, b) Photograph © 1983 The Metropolitan Museum of Art: 32; The Metropolitan Museum of Art, New York / The Bridgeman Art Library: 115; The Metropolitan Museum of Art, Backplate and rump defense; Gift of Bashford Dean, 1924; Arms; Mrs. Stephen V. Harkness Fund 1926 (24.179;26.188.1,2) Photograph © 1991 The Metropolitan Museum of Art: 45; The Metropolitan Museum of Art, Bequest of George C. Stone, 1935 (36.25.1297) Photograph © 1990 The Metropolitan Museum of Art: 73; Gift of Irwin Untermyer, 1964 (64.101.1492) Photograph C 1984 The Metropolitan Museum of Art: cover; Victor Minca / Art Resource, NY: 51; The Pierpont Morgan Library / Art Resource, NY: 100; © National Maritime Museum Picture Library: 98; Diego Velazquez, An Old Women Cooking Eggs / The National Gallery of Scotland: 117; National Palace Museum, Taipei / The Bridgeman Art Library: 19; The Nasser D. Khalili Collection of Islamic Art MTW 795: 23, 34; Nationalmuseet, Copenhagen / The Bridgeman Art Library: 50; Orlicka Galerie, Rychnov nad Kneznou, Czech Republic / The Bridgeman Art Library: 122; Ostasiatiska Museet / The Museum of Far Eastern Antiquites, Stockholm, NMOK-129. Karl Zetterstrom, photographer: 29; Polish National Tourist Office: 37; Prado, Madrid / The Bridgeman Art Library: 112; The Philadelphia Museum of Art / Art Resource, NY: 138; Réunion des Musées Nationaux/Art Resource, NY: 109, 126, 134, 139; Rumeli Hisari, Istanbul / The Bridgeman Art Library: 80; The Dr. Paul Singer Collection of Chinese Art of the Arthur M. Sackler Gallery of Art, Smithsonian Institution, a joint gift of the Arthur M. Sackler Foundation, Paul Singer, the A.M.S. Foundation for the Arts, Sciences and Humanities and the Childeren of Arthur M. Sackler, S2001.1.1-2: 136; Nicholas Sapieha / Art Resource, NY: 47; Scala / Art Resource, NY: 46, 67, 104, 114; Snark / Art Resource, NY: 2, 42, 55, 91, 119, 123; Nancy Toff: 57; Topkapi Palace Museum, Istanbul / The Bridgeman Art Library: 16, 79, 87; Vanni / Art Resource, NY: 88, 95, 102; Victoria & Albert Museum, London / Art Resource, NY: 62, 64, 66, 68, 69; Werner Forman / Art Resource, NY: 21, 27, 60, 142; Lisbon, Portugal, Ken Welsh / The Bridgeman Art Library: 97; Courtesy of Map Collection, Yale University Library: 53

MARJORIE WALL BINGHAM has taught history and English at the high school and junior high school levels and more recently served as an adjunct faculty member in the Graduate School for Liberal Studies at Hamline University. A founder of the Organization of History Teachers, the National Council for History Education, and the Upper Midwest Women's History Center, she has also served on several national committees for history in the schools. The co-author of 10 books on women's history, including *Women and the Constitution*, her work has led her to uncover the roles of women in numerous societies, past and present, from around the world. Her dedication to education earned her the Nancy Roelker Award from the American Historical Association in 1994. She lives in Minnesota.

BONNIE G. SMITH is Board of Governors Professor of History at Rutgers University. She has edited a series for teachers on Women's and Gender History in Global Perspective for the American Historical Association and has served as chair of the test development committee for the Advanced Placement examination in European history. Professor Smith is the author of many books on European, comparative, and women's history, among them *Confessions of a Concierge* and *Imperialism: A History in Documents*. She is co-author of *The Making of the West: Peoples and Cultures*, editor in chief of the forthcoming Oxford encyclopedia on women in world history, and general editor of an Oxford world history series for high school students and general readers.